Indian English Fiction since Independence: Readings from the Periphery

Indian English Fiction since Independence: Readings from the Periphery

Edited by

G.A. Ghanshyam
Prasanta Chakraborty

Prestige Books International
New Delhi: Sydney

Published by
Prestige Books International
New Delhi 110 060
email: prestigebooks@gmail.com

Associate Office
60/29-45 Parramatta Road,
Concord, NSW 2137
Australia

Printed in India

Contents

Preface

Indian English fiction reached its maturity within a short span of time after independence. In comparison to other regional literatures, this seems to be a sharp rise, and with good reasons! Indian English fiction has to compete with other English literatures outside its own political territory to capture the hearts of more and more English readers. Also, diasporic writings have contributed a lot towards its regular growth. And let's not forget, globalisation has also had a direct impact on this variety of Indian literature. In addition to this are the tough challenges it has to face all through from the regional literatures, for which there are already dedicated readers. Due to its unique features of flexibility, this variety of Indian language can accommodate as many numbers of socio-political and cultural issues in this type of Indian fiction. Consequently, the takers of this type are increasing throughout the world. It is, so to speak, looking at the world and having a taste of its diversity through the windows of Indian English fiction. As regards literary taste, Indian English attracts a plethora of critical theories as it is one of the few languages in the world to accommodate both the Oriental and the Occidental scholastic literary theories, both ancient and modern, to study literature. As a matter of fact, Indian English fiction has played a significant role in bridging the gap between the East and West. Besides, identification with the common man and the post-independence despair found an expression in the Indian novel. Some of the major issues that perturbed many post-independence Indian novelists are the problems of partition and its tragic after-effect, the use of Indian myths to depict modern

Indian life, handling of the problem of the minorities by the government in post-independence India, socio-economic predicaments like corruption, inefficiency, poverty and cumulative misery, psychiatrical disorder of the teenagers and old men alike, picture of Indians—within the country and abroad, of the Dalits' life and life in the North-East etc.

It is said that the exceptional expansion of Indian English literature began in 1981 with Salman Rushdie's *Midnight's Children*. As acknowledged by many, it was a game-changer as far as the growth of Indian fiction is concerned. Rushdie's success story was appropriately followed by equally talented and versatile writers like Amitav Ghosh, V.S. Naipaul, Rohinton Mistry, Bapsi Sidhwa, Amish Tripathi, Chitra Banerjee Divakaruni, Makarand Paranjape et al. Throughout the decade of 1990s, we find a boom in Indian English fiction writing, with many outstanding novels from Indian authors representing various new themes, genres and sections of society in their wide-ranging works.

The sociological troubles in the country gave rise to alienation, hardly a theme in the pre-independence period, which became a major concern after the independence. Effects of the Western economy and culture also contributed in this regard. The North East, which had remained neglected for so long, found a strong and clear voice through it. The West proved to be a potential agency, especially for the growth of Indian diasporic literature, but Indian myths also remained a dominant mode of expression in many of the novels and short stories, thereby giving importance to the narrative techniques of Indian classics. The present anthology is a selection of research articles discussing the multi-dimensional aspects of Indian English fiction, a reflection of its varied culture and literary tradition.

This anthology opens up with an article on diasporic literature "Defining and Re-Defining Diasporic Writing in English" by Somdatta Mandal. It begins with the initial problem of labelling a diasporic writer and then goes on to discuss the issues, problems and possibilities of Indian diasporic writing. The issues include cross-cultural conflicts/dilemmas, especially in areas where difference in generation, gender and sexuality intersect.

Following this, is the article by Bidhan Chandra Pal who critically assesses the physical and mental status of Mr. Biswas in *A House for Mr. Biswas.* In his article, Bidhan Chandra Pal shows that how a man like Mr. Biswas is destined to live in a derelict land. Society offers very little possibilities to men like Mr. Biswas. Tulsidom as a symbol of tyrant force plays a significant role here in the life of a man like Mr. Biswas.

Mr. Biswas left his own country, India, to settle in West Indies. But his experience there under the domination of Tulsidom is as bad as that of the slaves. The article assesses the psychic problem that a diasporic like Mr. Biswas had to face in a Creole society bereft of his own religion and culture. Mr. Biswas tries to cope up with the upcoming society, better identified as a hotchpotch society, with a mixture of different cultures, language and religion. But he could not do so and had to leave the land not for India but for the promised land of London.

This anthology has three papers on the immediate effect of partition theme, while the fourth one is on the books where two of the three novelists, Amitav Ghosh and Salman Rushdie, are making a post-mortem analysis of the partition and its impact in the post-independence era. Khushwant Singh, the third one, depicts the horrors of partition. In "Glimpses of Partition: Interrogating Insanity and Religiosity: Sadat Hasan Manto's 'Toba Tek Singh' and 'Mozel'," Olivia Sarkar attempts a discussion based on the experiences and sufferings of the common men and women consequent to partition. Urvashi Butalia writes that the political partition of India caused one of the great human convulsions of history. Never before or ever since had so many people exchanged their homes and countries so quickly. As one looks back, partition is more than a political divide—it is also a division of hearts. But this is not reflected in the written history.

In "Recovering for Whose Sake: Studying Abduction and Recovery in the Context of Partition in Rajinder Singh Bedi's 'Lajwanti,'" Somdev Banik studies the facets of partition violence on women. The paper raises the issue of double dispossession of women in the act of independence and also attempts to analyze the necessity of the nations to recover their 'abducted' subject citizens from the hands of the enemy.

In yet another article "Presentation of Loss and Trauma in Bapsi Sidhwa's *Ice-Candy Man,*" Pratap Dev discusses how the world around Lenny Sethi changes amidst partition. Bapsi Sidhwa's *Ice-Candy Man* is the narration of the experiences of an eight-year-old lame girl, Lenny when there was a sudden change in the atmosphere. The usual harmony of the people of different religions is soon replaced by violence, suspicion and disbelief at the approach of the partition. All the characters in the novel suffer loss which ultimately creates trauma in their mind. Although the article is on a Pakistani novelist, yet this has been considered for two reasons. Firstly, the theme refers to the period prior to India becoming trifurcated—India, West Pakistan and East Pakistan. Secondly, it gives an opportunity to be familiar with the attitude of a Pakistani novelist on the partition-issue.

Khushwant Singh's portrayal of the partition-related violence in *A Train to Pakistan* is not the same as it is found in Salman Rushdie's *Midnight's Children* which is the only novel to cover both the 1947 partition that divided India into two separate nations, and the later division in 1971, when East and West Pakistan turned into Pakistan and Bangladesh. It is basically an acknowledgement of the enormity of the error of the partition and manifests the bitter irony of the intended purpose of partition. In *Shadow Lines*, Amitav Ghosh is more concerned about the aftermath of partition. For Ghosh, the partition event has served as a source to explore concepts like 'freedom' and 'nationalism' that were associated with the idea of partition and to question the very idea of border by introducing the concept of borderless boundary. This is what Nirmalya Bhattacharyya studies in his article "Partition: A Metaphor of Mourning, Memory & Identity Crisis in Post-Independence Indian English Fiction" to show how the same theme has been handled differently by the three great novelists.

There are three articles on the impact of Indian myth in Indian English fiction. In her article, "Reinventing Myth: A Study of *The Palace of Illusions* by Chitra Banerjee Divakaruni," Banani Chakraborty critically analyzes how Chitra Banerjee Divakaruni has tried her hand in re-inventing the mythical epic *Mahabharata* in her novel *The Palace of Illusions.* Divakaruni reflects the horror and unavoidable destruction caused by war. *The Palace of Illusions* is rather a re-invention of the epic in the sense that the writer encapsulates the occurrences of the epic in the novelistic genre and inspires the modern readers to find parallels with the modern situation.

In his paper, "Mingled Yarn: History and Myth in Amish Tripathi's *The Immortals of Meluha,* Part 1 of *The Shiva Trilogy,*" Partha Sarathi Gupta investigates into the reasons behind the recurrence of history and mythology in Indian-English fiction. Amish Tripathi explores the undercurrents of alternate narratives within the grand narratives of mythology and recorded history of ancient, medieval and modern India. This paper takes up Amish Tripathi's best-seller *The Immortals of Meluha, Part 1,* to explore the conscious attempts on the part of contemporary Indian-English novelists to represent the 'inescapably Indian' through alternate modes of discourse in fiction writing, traditionally entrenched in Western notions of realism.

Indian epic and myth contributed a lot in the development of Indian English novel. Rama Chowdhury focuses in her article "*The Great Indian Novel*: A Study in Narrative" on how the lofty epic framework of the *Mahabharata* is brilliantly used to relate the political story of a nation. *The Great Indian Novel* transforms the family saga of Kauravas and Pandavas into a modern saga of India's most significant historical period. Myth and reality are interwoven, rendering it into a grand piece of retrospect, revelation, reversal and retrieval.

In another study, "Raj Kamal Jha's *The Blue Bedspread*: A Psychoanalytical Study," C.L. Khatri evaluates and explores the thematic and artistic aspects of Raj Kamal Jha's novel from a psychoanalytical perspective rather than a socio-cultural perspective, since it is a character-oriented novel.

In "Makarand Paranjape's *The Narrator: A Novel*—A Psychoanalytical Study," Tamojoy Brahma adopts the Freudian model of Id, Ego and Super-ego respectively to analyse the character of Rahul. Tamojoy Brahma observes that the central concern of the novel is to represent a potential writer's anxiety about the making of a narrative or a novel. The paper, while taking into consideration the Freudian model of Id, Ego and Super-ego, also highlights the Deleuze and Félix Guattarian model of the schizo-analysis—that "schizophrenia" embraces "a positive process"—a rhetorical trope to write a fiction.

In his article "Aravind Adiga's *The White Tiger*: A Reading of the Novel in the Light of Hegel and Nietzsche's Concepts of Master-Slave Relationship," Anup Kumar Dey observes that the novel portrays an unattractive image of India rattled by poverty, underdevelopment and corruption and is also an interesting study of the master-servant relationship, which may be analyzed from the context of Hegelian Master-Slave Dialectic as well as Friedrich Nietzsche's concept of Master-Slave morality.

A new dimension of literary criticism that is presently in vogue is eco-criticism that undertakes a critical study of the relationship of man with nature. This is what Dipankar Chakrabarti does in his article "Ecological Degradation and Identity Crisis of the Minority: A Study of Rohinton Mistry's *A Fine Balance*." In the novel Mistry has portrayed the man-nature relationship with utmost sensitivity and depth through his characters drawn from the Parsi community. The existential crisis generated by partition and its subsequent after-effect in the form of massive ecological degradation that they confront in their personal, social and national life constitutes the central concern of the novel. This article has been clubbed with the articles on the subalterns.

In her article, "Indian Novel: An Epoch-making Genre—Agent for Socio-Psycho-National Reforms," Adwitiya Gope studies Krupabai Satthianadhan's *Saguna*, Khushwant Singh's *A Train to Pakistan*, Salman Rushdie's *Midnight's Children* with occasional references to some other Indian English novels to show how the emergence of Indian English novel, from its introduction under the aegis of the 19th century British colonial policies through the 1980s, worked as an agency for socio-psycho-national reforms.

The importance of the graphic novel genre in Indian context lies in the fact that it depicts 'Indianness' through both text and image. In her article "Exploring Image-Text Relations in a Post-Independence Indian English Graphic Novel *The Barn Owl's Wondrous Capers,"* Archita Gupta explores the image-text relation in an Indian English graphic novel that enables contextualization of 'local' space and gives a concrete picture of colonial Calcutta through illustrations. The novel, simultaneously, is also a postmodern dig at conventional historiography and the paper explores the nuances of this text at multiple levels.

Although Indian English writing faced a lot of opposition from different corners both before and after independence because of the preconceived idea that the language is elitist in nature and is therefore separated from the masses, the Indian English fiction writers have attained a prestigious place in the world literature, especially after the 1980s. They have brought laurels to the nation by winning several prestigious international literary awards. The impact of globalisation has transformed this once elitist language into the language of the masses.

The contributors are hopeful that this volume will be patronized by the academics, scholars and students. Constructive suggestions are requested from well-wishers to improve the quality of the content and presentation in their future endeavours.

I am personally grateful to Dr. R.K. Dhawan of Prestige, New Delhi to kindly consider publishing the articles. His encouragement and interest in academic activities are par excellence. I am sincerely encouraged by his kindness. I also admire the efforts of staff at Prestige Press for giving this volume an excellent shape.

1 June 2013

G.A. Ghanshyam
Prasanta Chakraborty

Of Defining and Re-Defining Diasporic Indian Writing in English

SOMDATTA MANDAL

Taking the cue from the noted Kannada writer's remark, it is a matter of peculiar distress to many bibliophiles that most of the successful Indian books of the past few decades have not only been written in English but authored by Indians, or the children of Indians, living outside the country. 'Can it be true that Indian writing that endlessly rich, complex and problematic entity, is to be represented by a handful of writers who write in English, who live in England or America and whom one might have met at a party' wondered novelist Amit Choudhury in the picador book of modern Indian literature; 'yes' wrote Salman Rushdie in the Vintage book of Indian writing. the ironic proposition that India's best writing since independence may have been done in the language of the departed imperialists,' he said, 'is simply too much for some folks to bear.' Though the status of all diasporic Indian writers is not the same that many of them reside outside the nation state of India and have been awarded literary prizes and astronomical sums as advance complicate the situation further. This paper will begin with the initial problem of labelling a diasporic writer and then go on to discuss the issues, problems and possibilities of Indian diasporic writing. This will include issues of cross-cultural conflict /dilemmas especially in areas where difference in generation, gender and sexuality intersect. It will also focus on how voluntary diasporic subjects are different from those Indians whose lives were mapped by exile, mass migration and economic emigration.

As the beginning of the title suggests, this paper addresses a basic question as to what defines a diasporic writer. Is it the kind of writing that the author produces or the official identity of his/her home country as endorsed in his/her passport? This paper begins with the initial problem of labelling a diasporic writer and then goes on to discuss the issues, problems and possibilities of Indian English diasporic writing. This includes issues of cross-cultural conflicts/dilemmas especially in areas where difference in generations, gender and sexuality intersect. It also focuses on how more recent voluntary diasporic subjects are different from those Indians whose lives were mapped by exile, mass migration and economic emigration. The issues mentioned are meant to be merely highlighting some points to help with diasporic discourse/theory and they do not pretend to be exhaustive in covering the ground, the lie of land. Diasporas are defined vis-à-vis their relationship with their homelands, "as communities that actively maintain links with their cultures of origin, including creating and maintaining their own religious institutions, language schools, community centres, radio stations and so on" (5). Again diasporas are viewed in relation to the hostlands. An important issue which has hardly been addressed is when does a diaspora cease to be one? Is it the passage of time, a mindset, a cultural transformation, a feeling of being at home in the new land or citizenship that brings this about?

It is a matter of peculiar distress to many bibliophiles that most of the successful Indian books of the past few decades have not only been written in English but authored by Indians, or the children of Indians, living outside the country. "Can it be true that Indian writing, that endlessly rich, complex and problematic entity, is to be represented by a handful of writers who write in English, who live in England or America and whom one might have met at a party?" (xvii), wondered novelist Amit Chaudhuri in the *Picador Book of Modern Indian Literature*. "'Yes," wrote Salman Rushdie in his introduction to *The Vintage Book of Indian Writing 1947-1997,* "the ironic proposition that India's best writing since independence may have been done in the language of the departed imperialists is simply too much for some folks to bear" (xiv). Though the status of all diasporic Indian writers is not the same, the simple fact that many of them reside outside the nation-state of India and have been awarded literary prizes and astronomical sums as advance complicate the situation further. For example, the noted Kannada writer U.R. Ananthamurthy remarked, "A lot of new writers who get the kind of attention that Rushdie gives them are writers who write for export. It is a shame that in the whole world only Indian writers in English write for export." (2008:17).

Examining the themes of exile, identity, longing, displacement, race relations, rootlessness, and ultimately acceptance form the staple stuff of most novels written on the diasporic experience. In order to make sense of his present state, the writer revisits the past by taking recourse to memory and imagination. As Rushdie has noted in his 1984 essay "Imaginary Homelands," the migrant is always conscious of the fact that "it's my present that is foreign, and the past is home albeit a lost home in a lost city in the mists of lost time" (9). As the Indian abroad attempts to reclaim the lost home through the 'double filter' of 'time and migration,' the India that is remembered is no longer the one that was left behind, nor an invented one, but an *imagined* one:

> But if we do look back we must also do so in the knowledge . . . that our physical alienation from India almost inevitably means that we will not be capable of reclaiming precisely the things that were lost; that we will, in short, create fictions, not actual cities or villages, but invisible ones, imaginary homelands, Indias of the mind. (10)

This may largely be due, no doubt, to the fact that memory is notoriously unreliable, and frequently discontinuous, "It may be that when the Indian writer who writes from outside India tries to reflect that world, he is obliged to deal in broken mirrors, some of whose fragments have been irretrievably lost" (Rushdie 10-11). But the shards of the broken glass of nostalgia are not simply a mark of loss; reassembled, they can become, Rushdie believes, a useful tool for the novelist to portray the fractured and liminal exilic condition, the heap of broken images that also sums up contemporary life itself. Besides—and this is something Rushdie does not mention here—the remains of the past are also frequently assembled by the imagination to form a new, and kaleidoscopic design, one which, in Homi Bhabha's words, "does not merely recall the past as social cause or aesthetic precedent; it renews the past, refiguring it as a contingent 'in-between' space, that innovates and interrupts the performance of the present" (7). It is Stuart Hall who most effectively sums up this point in "Cultural Identity and Diaspora":

> Diaspora identities are those which are constantly producing and reproducing themselves anew, through transformation and difference. . . . It is because this New World is constituted for us as place, a narrative of displacement, that it gives rise so profoundly to a certain imaginary plenitude, recreating the endless desire to return to the 'lost origins.' . . . And yet, this 'return to the beginning' is like the imaginary in Lacan—it can neither be fulfilled nor requited, and hence in the beginning of the symbolic, of representation, the infinitely renewable source of desire, memory, myth, search, discovery. (223-37)

When we talk about diasporic Indian writing in English, we tend to see Indian expatriate individuals everywhere—scattered across several continents—as linked by a common heritage, history and racial descent. The first question that arises in our mind therefore is whether such a conception homogenizes difference and forms a kind of 'ethnic absolutism.' All the expatriates have not gone from the same racial, cultural and social circumstances; hence, their experiences cannot be homogenized. Broadly speaking, we can classify them into two groups as Diasporas in the West and Diasporas in the Asia-Pacific regions.

The formation of the Indian diaspora according to Amitav Ghosh "is not merely one of the most important demographic dislocations of modern times: it now represents an important force in world culture" (243) and can be classified, according to the critic Sudesh Mishra, as the 'sugar' and the 'masala' diaspora. There is also a distinction to be made between the old and the new Diasporas. "This distinction," according to Mishra, "is between, on the one hand, the semi-voluntary flight of indentured peasants to the non-metropolitan plantation colonies such as Fiji, Trinidad, Mauritius, South Africa, Malaysia, Surinam, and Guyana, roughly between the years 1830 and 1917; and on the other the late capital or postmodern dispersal of new migrants of all classes to thriving metropolitan centres, such as Australia, the United States, Canada and Britain." (276). This same classification is termed by other critics as 'forced diaspora' and 'voluntary diaspora.' Another critic and scholar, Vinay Lal, reiterates the same idea by calling it 'diaspora of labour' versus 'diaspora of longing.' For most of the old diasporic writers, there is an unease of the dislocated and the deracinated who either by choice or by compulsion have abandoned home in the country of their birth for a home in their adopted country. For the migrants of choice, on the other hand, the situation is totally different. They prefer to live in a kind of cosmopolitan globalised world where the markers of their borderless state have often to be invented.

The next important point that draws our attention is that diasporic individuals as subjects are generally marked by hybridity and heterogeneity—cultural, linguistic, ethnic, national—subjects defined by traversal of boundaries demarcating nation and expatriation. The double, even plural identity of the subject that is constructed from the expatriate experience is defined, not by essence or purity, but by the unavoidable heterogeneity and diversity. Identity in the postcolonial moment is less a matter of national affiliation than an issue of baggage, both figurative and literal, that one carries away from home. Unable to challenge the ruling establishment, writers usually prefer to tread on safer ground and speak of issues of alienation and acculturation. The categories of people in their fiction usually do not belong to either the traditionally opposed and fixed categories; each of which defines itself and the other. The feelings about India represent the deeply ambivalent emotions of the Indian 'intellectual exile': (to borrow Edward Said's idea) about the home they have left behind but cannot help return to again and again in memory and imagination; in their continuing search for identity, acculturation and belonging.

According to Amitav Ghosh, India is, and has always been, a pervasive emotional and psychological presence for "anybody anywhere who has even the most tenuous links with it and the mother country simply does not have the cultural means to cut him off" (250). Here I am reminded of what Himani Banerjee, a Canadian writer of Indian origin, stated in her introduction to a collection of essays published in 1995:

> I have spent half of my life in Toronto, coming no nearer and going no further than I did in the first few years. The journey of mine in Canada is like an arc, suspended, which has not found a ground yet. . . . Other than the language English, which I knew and taught, everything else was not only 'other' and alien, but also full of denial, rejection and sometimes . . . downright hatred (5)

It therefore becomes clear that expatriation does not transcend differences of race, class, gender, and sexuality, nor can it stand alone as an epistemological or historical category of analysis, separate and distinct from these interrelated categories. As A.L. McLeod points out, diasporic writers have variously described themselves as migrants, plural, hybrid, expatriate, immigrant—every individual investing these words with personal and restrictive connotations. Moreover, these metaphors express not only spatial disorientation but also ideological and existential fragmentation. Also, there are varying degrees of significance of the originary homeland for the second generation and the generations succeeding it, born and brought up as they are in the diasporic context across the globe. Question arises as to how they differ from the first/immigrant generation in relating to their cultural heritage. Longing for roots is inherent in all generations of expatriates. Whereas the first generation usually suffers from more nostalgia and desire for the return to the roots, the subsequent generations find the originary land necessary to understand their confused diasporic status better. For example, some of Jhumpa Lahiri's short stories and her novel *The Namesake* show the trend. Listening to her mother's stories and regularly visiting her relatives in Calcutta gave her writing the correct blend of intimacy and distance that is necessary for a good writer.

Labelling or defining diasporic Indian fiction writers in English has posed several problems. Emmanuel S. Nelson defines the Indian diaspora as the "historical and contemporary presence of people of Indian sub-continental origin in other areas of the world" (x). Many are first generation expatriates who continue to consider India their true home, the place of their nurture, values, and extended families as well as their deepest sympathies and attachments. However, this is not universally the case; accommodated to overseas lifestyles, many members of the diaspora experience a distinct dissonance when reintroduced to their former sub-continental culture.

The critic Avtar Brah in *Cartographies of Diaspora*, emphasises on the desire for the homeland as recurrent theme in diasporic writing. Accordingly, he identifies four stages in the process of assimilation in the hostland. These are the tourist phase, the culture shock phase, the conformist phase and the assimilation phase. The diasporic nature of Indian writing in English once again has three visible sections. In the first category falls a writer like Bharati Mukherjee—one who detests the idea of being called the immigrant writer and considers herself mainstream American. Simplistically, she sees expatriates resisting assimilation, immigrants welcoming it. "For me," she says, "it is a movement away from the aloofness of expatriation to the exuberance of immigration" (Mukherjee 3). In the second category falls the whole group of writers like Amitav Ghosh, Vikram Seth, Gita Mehta, Kiran Desai and others who shuttle between different continents. Within this group, some write about their immigrant experiences, while others physically living there write on the exoticism of their home country or of characters who go as aliens and try to fit into the western world. Sunetra Gupta is a case in point. Born in Calcutta she now lives in Oxford and her novels *Memories of Rain* (1992) and *A Sin of Colour* (1999) are set in both Calcutta and Oxford. Living in London, Meera Syal believes that the duality and conflict makes one want to express oneself and that is why her generation is so outspoken.

The most complicated case is the third category of writers whose origin is India but have no connections as such with the country. Bidisha Bandopadhyay (who incidentally never writes her surname) is a second-generation Bengali writer born and brought up in England. Her debut novel *Seahorses* (1997) is an urban pageant about three young British men and in no way even remotely connected to India. Another interesting example is that of Jhumpa Lahiri whose *Interpreter of Maladies* (2000) took the literary world by storm. Bill Buford, the literary editor of *The New Yorker* catapulted her into limelight when he included her in his list of "the twenty best young fiction writers in America today" (6). Born in London, raised in Rhode Island, Connecticut, and presently living in Brooklyn, New York, Jhumpa set some of her stories in Calcutta because of "a necessary combination of distance and intimacy" and in an interview to Radhika S. Shankar she said: "I went to Calcutta neither as a tourist nor as a former resident—a valuable position, I think, for a writer. . . . I learnt to observe things as an outsider and yet I also knew that, as different as Calcutta is from Rhode Island, I belonged there in some fundamental way. In the ways I didn't seem to belong in the US" (Lahiri 1999).

Kiran Desai, whose debut novel *Hullabaloo in the Guava Orchard* (1998) found extraordinary welcome on both sides of the Atlantic and who received the Man Booker Prize for *The Inheritance of Loss* (2006), shuttles between New York and Cambridge and even goes off to a remote retreat in Mexico along with her mother for literary inspiration. We all know that Salman Rushdie played a significant role in catapulting her into fame even before her first novel had seen the light of day. So when Kiran tells an interviewer that there is "a cosy community of Indian writers" now in New York—people like Suketu Mehta, Jhumpa Lahiri, Amitav Ghosh, Salman Rushdie—who "talk to each other very often" and "when [they] get tired or need a break, [they] meet up and cook together and go out for drinks together" (Kiran Desai's interview with Nabanita Sircar, *India Today*, October 30, 2006. 82), we feel tempted to ask whether they also discuss the ways and means of securing good publishers in the west, as well as the strategies of competing for various literary prizes. After winning the Booker Prize for *The Inheritance of Loss,* Desai took her diasporic status as an advantageous position and ecstatically stated in the same interview to Nabanita Sircar, "The Indian diaspora is a wonderful place to write from and I am lucky to be part of it" (Bhatia). Although Kiran has not lived in India since she was fourteen, she returns to the family home in Delhi every year, primarily to meet her father. As the BBC News story tells us, she also returned to India to write parts of the novel: "I went back to write the Indian bits in India, so it wasn't entirely from a distance" (Bhatia). So she is able to mix a sense of intimacy and distance in her writing, something that brings her close to a writer like Jhumpa Lahiri. Desai elsewhere also explains to Laura Barton why she had to base her story in the India of the 1980s and how she realized that she would have to return to India only when she began writing about the immigrant experience in New York:

> I find myself at a disadvantage because India has changed, moved on. I go every ear, yet it belongs to Indian authors living in India. The subject belongs to them. So the only way I could put this book together was to go back to the India of the 1980s, when I left. (Barton)

To Nabanita Sircar she reiterates "I left India in the 1980s. It was different then. Now I am envious of writers in India. So much is happening there. It makes me and my writer friends often wonder what to do next." (*ibid.*). *The Inheritance of Loss* is a novel, which according to the author herself, concerns with "the enormous anxiety of being a foreigner" (300).

As we are all aware, the labelling of diasporic Indian English writers is a problem indeed. Can we consider a writer Indian by virtue of his/her birth alone? Does the writer remain an Indian writer if he/she writes in the voice of a western persona? Is it the literature that makes a writer Indian or his/her passport? Whether the syllabi of an Indian university can include writers from all these three categories still remain a debatable point but the way all these novelists' names are used at random by critics to define diasporic Indian Writing in English as well makes things complicated indeed. Though a diasporic Indian writer can be very serious about issues of his/her homeland, the question still remains whether writers living outside India forfeit the right to comment on behalf of an entire nation or not.

In his analysis on diasporas and the transnational experience, James Clifford is careful to qualify his assertions about the identities of diasporic groups, claiming that we should be wary of constructing our working definitions of diasporas around 'an ideal type' and that a more 'polythetic' definition is necessary. (Clifford). The immediate definition he sees as insufficient is one posed by William Safran in the inaugural issue of the journal *Diaspora* in 1991. Safran identifies six defining characteristics of diasporic individuals and their 'dilemmas': they have a history of dispersal; they possess myths and memories of the homeland;

they experience alienation in the host country; they have a desire for eventual return and ongoing support for the homeland; and they have a collective identity that is defined by this relationship. (Safran 84). Clifford goes on to contradict himself when he asserts that diasporas are different from ethnic communities because they are not 'here to stay': there is always a tension between living here and desiring or remembering another place. Clifford suggests moving beyond Safran's limited theorization of transnational diasporic communities: by assuming diasporic individuals do not feel as if they are in the host-nation to stay, is to constrict the complexities of such an experience. It is exactly such constrictions that most diasporic Indian writers in English seek to counteract and challenge. Here we can also reiterate and apply the question that Safran poses for further exploration at the end of his article, "Is there an ideal type of relationship between the country of origin and diaspora community that is contingent on their respective roles? And under what conditions are these roles inverted?" (Safran 95).

In the gifted writers, the cross-cultural conflicts/dilemmas are generally disrupted and complicated in productive ways, especially in areas where differences in generations, gender and sexuality intersect—as Meera Syal in Britain and Jhumpa Lahiri in the USA. This points to a trend or a pattern in the future of Indian diaspora also. Both Syal and Lahiri write from their own experiences of living abroad as a second-generation immigrant in a multicultural society. An Indian by descent, the Kenyan-born, Tanzania-raised, US-educated, and a Canadian by citizenship since 1978, M.G. Vassanji is a writer who falls somewhere in between the two categories. Like Neil Bisoondath and Michael Ondaatje, he is an Indian expatriate separated from the subcontinent by generations. Talking of his career and of his roots, what Vassanji says to his interviewer Gene Carey makes it clear that the past always haunts the present and future of all these writers:

> Once you come here, cross the oceans, there's no going back. There is a psychological belonging to East Africa, particularly Tanzania. You need something to hold on. . . . I went back to Tanzania in 1989 after 19 years. It is part of my soul. The other part is India, which I visited for the first time in 1993. My father had never been to India, the land of my forefathers. After that I have visited India a couple of times. (Carey)

Another aspect that perplexes us relates to how voluntary diasporic subjects can be different from those whose lives were mapped by exile, refugee camps, mass migration and economic emigration. How do constructions of nation and diaspora differ in various trans-migrational groups like exiles, fugitives, refugees, immigrants and migrants? The idea of inhabiting many spaces but belonging to none creates a sense of double vision in many of these subjects. Sometimes these forced migrations change the nature of things, like shifting of loyalty. What is interesting is that in order to forget the trauma that they have faced, in most cases these forced migrants prefer to remain totally silent about it. The literature of the Partition of India is a reminder of this kind of a situation. The result often leads to eulogizing or romanticizing without any direct reference to socio-political issues. Creating family memoirs or coming-of-age stories that look at the past with affection and understanding, the writers thus try to show that the hopes and dreams of the Indian exiles are essentially the same as those of the Europeans who went to the New World. Amitav Ghosh's *The Sea of Poppies* (2008) tells us about the trials, tribulations and adventures of the 'girmits' (coolies) who crossed the Kala Pani in search of new jobs in the different British plantations across far spread colonies. The only similarity between these people and those who migrated outside India by choice lies in their dreams of a better life.

The life of the rural poor, small-town life in the region, and the life in the mega cities of the subcontinent have all been represented in English literature emanating from India. The alienated consciousness of the writer using the English language is another important factor. But since the late 1970s and early 1980s; after expatriation and immigration to the west, the trauma of uprooting, the diasporic consciousness and the loss of 'home' and identity have preoccupied Indian Writing in English. To what extent does the 'old country' function as a framework and regulate the transplanted identities within the diaspora? All expatriate writers continuously ponder on the question of where is 'home.' On the one hand, it is a mythic place of desire in the diasporic imagination and in this sense it is a place of no return. On the other hand, home is also the lived experience of a locality. Regardless of their emotional attachments and legal status, they are alienated from the dominant group. In an interview given to S. Prasannarajan about his novel *Shalimar the Clown* (2005), Salman Rushdie clearly states that there is no escape from India:

> I have never written a novel without an Indian central character and don't expect to do so any time soon. I am sure that some novels will veer away from India while others swing back towards it. That's inevitable in the work of a writer whose experience is divided among several different worlds. (Rushdie, *India Today*, September 12, 2005)

Bharati Mukherjee had to come back to her roots in Bengal while setting *Desirable Daughters* and in her latest novel *Miss New India* (2011) all the events take place in a small town in Bihar and the IT hub of Bangalore. The 'old country' thus always serves as a ready referral at any point of creativity. Jhumpa Lahiri admits to Vibhuti Patel that there is less of a divide between American culture and Indian because of the greater access and communication channels, "But I have observed a sense of emotional exile in my parents and in their friends that I feel can never go away." On the other hand, "the problem for children of immigrants, those with strong ties to their country of origin, is that they feel neither one thing nor the other.' . . . I've inherited my parent's preoccupations. It's hard to have parents who consider another place 'home'—even after living abroad for thirty years, India is home for them. We were always looking back so I never felt fully at home here." ("The Maladies of Belonging" *Newsweek International*, September 20, 1999. 80.).

Living in diaspora means living in forced or voluntary exile and living in exile usually leads to severe identity confusion, problems of identification and alienation from both, old and new cultures and homelands. In *Shame*, Rushdie generalizes:

> All migrants leave their pasts behind although some try to pack it into bundles and boxes—but on the journey something seeps out of the treasured mementoes and old photographs, until even their owners fail to recognize them, because it is the fate of immigrants to be stripped of history, to stand naked among the scorn of strangers upon whom they see the rich clothing, the brocades of continuity and the eyebrows of belonging. (Rushdie)

Therefore, most diasporic writing is suffused with identification consciousness and the problem of living in an alien society. As Rushdie has put it in *Imaginary Homelands*, the position of 'the exile or immigrant' is one of 'profound uncertainties' ("Imaginary Homelands"10). The diasporic person is at home neither in the West nor in India and is thus 'unhomed' (Homi Bhabha) in the most essential sense of the term. Thus the concept and interpretation of 'home' becomes vital in all kinds of diasporic writing. A good fictional example of this ambivalence is of Tha'mma in Amitav Ghosh's *The Shadow Lines* who is confused between going and coming home in Dhaka. So when diasporic writing tries to reflect real and imagined worlds, it "is obliged to deal in broken mirrors, some of whose fragments have been lost." ("Imaginary Homelands" 11)

Thus, we find roving, unsettled, alienated people in the fictive world of contemporary diasporic writers yearning for a real or imaginary homeland, a permanent or temporary return. However, this could also be seen as the strength of diasporic texts—

that they are incomplete, the fact that they do not claim to offer the ultimate truth—the fact that they deal with alternatives rather than essentials. It is these alternative histories and narratives that Salman Rushdie's texts have offered from *Midnight's Children* (1981) down to *The Ground beneath Her Feet* (2000). In *Imaginary Homelands*, Rushdie extends his perception of migrant writers as endowed with a double/plural, insider/outside perspective, whose hybrid predicament can be universalized into art with a globally accepted theme. In her introduction to *Darkness,* Bharati Mukherjee distinguishes between 'expatriate' and 'immigrant':

> In my fiction and in my Canadian experience, immigrants were lost souls, put upon and pathetic. Expatriates on the other hand, knew all too well who and what they were, and what foul hate had befallen them. Like V.S. Naipaul in whom I imagined a model, I tried to explore state-of-the-art expatriation. (3)

Closely associated with this phenomenon is media hype. Aggressive marketing blitz, huge advances; book launch parties, rave reviews and other frills have no doubt helped Indian writing in English to hit the market. This hype and media blitzkrieg created by publishers for an Indian writer making it big in the West is rarely witnessed in the case of Indian translations. Anita Desai, who started writing in the 1950s and 1960s and was then stationed in Delhi, later moved out to live permanently in the United States. Reminiscing about 'Modern Indian Writing,' she states how the whole phenomenon has now moved from the cave to a bazaar. Her earlier writing experience was "an act of solitary confinement and the actual existence of writers no more than a rumour spread by their books." It was "like being deep inside a dark cave, quite alone." She further added:

> The picture changed abruptly, dramatically, in 1981 when a book called *Midnight's Children* appeared on the scene like a thunderbolt and the author was sent to India on that until then unknown exercise, a book tour. It was the combination of a book that proved

> that Indian English was a language in itself, capable of presenting serious and important ideas with vigour and originality . . . and of the author as a personality, a living personality, that changed the Indian scene overnight. . . . Things have never been the same since. (8)

Here we are reminded of the media hype that accompanied *The God of Small Things* (1997) after it won the Booker Prize. When Vikram Seth received more than 3.1 crore rupees in advance for the US, British and Indian rights of *A Suitable Boy* (1993), it trumpeted the arrival of a literary cult—the idolization of writers who gained recognition in the West. Along with their astronomical advance amounts, they all seem to try out their luck in this Cinderella syndrome. As Bill Buford wryly comments, "It showed publishers in the West that books by an Indian writer could sell" (7). So getting recognition from the West first is nothing new for Indian writers in English. As Anita Desai pointed out further:

> there is now such a din in the publishing world that it is beginning to resemble that hoary cliché, the Eastern bazaar. The clamour—agents! contracts! royalties! awards!—make the words *literature, writing, books* fade to whispers. (8-9)

Diasporic Indian writers in English have often been criticized of writing for the western audience, and with an eye towards bagging a Booker or a Commonwealth Writer's award. Expatriate writers have often blended or juxtaposed the earlier formulaic pattern mentioned. Rushdie's use of magic realism mode has also been successfully found in Divakaruni's first novel, *The Mistress of Spices* (1997) and her later fictional work, *The Queen of Dreams* (2004). History, in addition to magic realism, has been the major preoccupation of the recent expatriate Indian writer in English. There is a view that many of our contemporary novelists writing in English are overburdened with history and in novelist Shashi Deshpande's opinion, the novels are so full of details from Indian history that they end up sagging under its weight. One novelist whose novels do not suffer from this excess as alleged by Deshpande is Rohinton Mistry, who has been living in Canada for several decades now. His *A Fine Balance* (1995) attempts to locate the lives of its characters in a historical context, i.e. the personal is seen in relation to the general. His *Such a Long Journey* (1996) follows a similar pattern and explores into areas of human experience that was hitherto only tangentially touched upon. Amitav Ghosh is another novelist who explores the relationships between historical processes and human destiny. In his novel *The Shadow Lines* (2005), Ghosh successfully interweaves personal history with a nation's destiny giving us a poignant story of the Partition. Another direct result of the globalized world is found in the way some diasporic novels are set in a contemporary de-territorialized world spanning different continents. Thus the characters in Amitav Ghosh's *The Shadow Lines* or Sunetra Gupta's *Moonlight into Marzipan* (1995) elude a sort of cosmopolitan identity that is usually not found in Indian English fiction in general.

This leads us to the use of language and what creative purpose must have been meant to be achieved with the inclusion of Indian words in expatriate Indian writing when they actually create a barrier in the understanding for the international reader. Rushdie's 'chutneyfication' of Indian English is all too well-known. In contemporary diasporic as well as resident Indian writers, the use of vernacular words without references or explanations too has definitely become a new fad. Indian Writing in English has come a long way from the use of words with glossary at the end explaining their meanings; to use of words in italics without any glossary; to the present state when non-English words are no longer even italicized. The writers are doing this kind of exoticization with a sort of vengeance now.

A substantial number of Indian expatriates have several homelands since they have changed places from India, Africa, Britain, and Far East and so on after long periods of stay in each place. So how does critical discourse treat such multiple acts of expatriation? The task of labelling a writer is that of the academic and not of the writer. We tend to categorize them under different groups, so much so that the same writer might feature in different categories. Take for example the case of Bharati Mukherjee. We can find her mentioned under the category American writer (her own preferred choice), Asian-American writer, Canadian writer, Indian writer in English, South Asian Diasporic writer and Postcolonial writer. For many other writers who have undergone multiple migrations, the case is the same. Uma Parameswaran calls it the plight of the 'Trishanku'—the mythic character from the *Ramayana* who went 'embodied' to heaven but had to settle at an intermediate third space, midway between the earth and paradise. In his novel, *The In-Between World of Vikram Lall* (2003), Moyez Vassanji calls this state of being as 'in-betweenness' where the protagonist confesses, "I am the guilty one in the middle, the perilous in-between," (279), hence never to be trusted. The characters in this deeply textured novel carry their histories with them wherever they go.

Is it possible to draw a line of distinction between authentic projections of Indian reality and the exoticized/stereotyped versions of the same as depicted by diasporic Indian writers? The problem is rather complicated because there has been a constant critical refrain about marketing the margins. Some writers avoid direct socio-political issues and tread on safe ground by either romanticizing the mother country that they have left behind or create what Naipaul calls physical India versus the 'India of the mind.' Besides that, the most important question that might be asked in this context is whether the writer living in the West ceases to be considered as spokesperson of a nation or not. While the exoticization of India as a land of princes, elephants, snake charmers has long been over, other forms of overt or covert exoticization still persist. Take the case of Arundhati Roy's *The God of Small Things*. It won the Booker Prize in October 1997 and in the 'Travel Watch' section of the international *Time* magazine in March the next year; Ayemenem in Kerala was marketed as a must-see travel destination because it was the setting of the book, part of 'God's Own Country.' The commodification of India in the global literary marketplace is most visible in the anti-realistic representations in Rushdie's later fiction, as well as in the more realistic depictions in Bharati Mukherjee and Chitra Banerjee Divakaruni's works. Against this, we also have Amitav Ghosh's authentic descriptions of the Sunderbans in *The Hungry Tide* (2005), and the blending of real and imagined Calcutta in *The Calcutta Chromosome* (1996).

This leads to another question. How do writers like Ashis Gupta and Michael Ondaatje, who have written about subjects unrelated to their bicultural/transcultural experience, answer the question of authenticity? Or, is this to be viewed as deliberate creative evasion of the delimiting hold of hyphenated label? About his 1989 book *The Gunny Sack,* M.G. Vassanji says that he had put a lot of his emotional baggage in the novel. "We all carry the past inside us in some way," (168), says the narrator of his novel *The In-Between World of Vikram Lall.* For most expatriate writers therefore, the home culture usually provides ready material for the publisher to accept. Question arises what is the status of an expatriate writer who does not write about the bicultural or transcultural experience. In their urge to avoid the label of an ethnic writer, some of them often write about mainstream issues that are not even remotely connected with problems of alienation and acculturation. An interesting example is that of Abha Dawesar, whose debut novel *The Three of Us* (2003) is not what we usually expect from a 26-year-old immigrant Indian writer in the United States of America. She creates a story that shrewdly explores sexual dependency from the perspective of a white male investment banker in Manhattan, New York, whose affairs range from having sex with his boss as well as his wife, all neatly timed with the help of a mini-planner. In an article called "India Away from Home," Dawesar explains her predicament and raises several pertinent questions that can be applied to many others as well:

> My novel was about and in the voice of a young man: Andre Bernard. A white man. A gay man. An American. The book was not of India in any sense of the term. Can I be considered an Indian writer by virtue of my birth alone? Do I remain an Indian writer if I write in the voice of a white American man? Is it my literature that makes me India or my passport? This class of questions will gain in significance as diasporic writing speaks in more and more tongues. (Dawesar 31)

Before concluding, I would like to reiterate that in the postcolonial transnational scenario of the twenty-first century, the problem of labelling diasporic Indian Writing in English is still there and cannot be solved too easily. For the writers seem to remain contented to be labelled simply as 'writers' and it is we academics who try to compartmentalize them into neatly formed Chinese boxes for our convenience. For example, while some reporters have simply called Kiran Desai 'a writer,' *Times of India* called her an 'Indian-origin writer'; *Wikipedia* termed her as 'a citizen of India and a permanent Resident of the U.S.,' the Booker Prize committee described her as 'the Indian-born writer,' *The Hindu* called her 'an Indian writer,' and the reporter of *The Telegraph*, 'the New-York based writer.' Ravi Dayal, admitting to being a small publisher, is not sure whether marketing strategy is of paramount importance when it comes to building the profile of an author. He believes that critical readership in India has come of age and the readers are the best judges of a work. Looking at the present day scenario, Amitav Ghosh's point of view becomes very relevant in this perspective:

> It seems to me that this notion of the periphery has now expanded to include the diaspora. That is why the opinions of the diaspora are so significant to India: it is that part of itself which is both hos-

> tage and representative in the world outside—it is the mirror in which modern India seeks to know itself. (250)

In an essay entitled "The Historical Formation of Indian English Literature," Vinay Dharwadker mentions how migrant and itinerant writers have energized Indian Writing in English in most of its historical phases as well as in the early postcolonial decades. He identifies four or five zones of contact that have provided a social framework for Indian English literary culture since the late eighteenth century, the principal change being that the zones are now geographically located overseas. First in its foreign setting it has contributed generally as well as concretely to the growth and dissemination of Indian women's writing and intellectual work across international borders. This fragmented yet interlinked community has produced many of the newest authors of Indian origin in English, besides serving as an extensive, enthusiastic international readership for contemporary Indian English writing.

Secondly, the zone of marriage and family has altered a lot in its internal structure resulting in varied interracial and intercultural social-sexual relations and has left its mark in the racial, cultural and sexual aspects of diasporic Indian-English writing. Interracial marriage in the diaspora mediates the work, for instance of Bharati Mukherjee, Meena Alexander, Sunetra Gupta, and Sujata Bhatt among women writers, and of Salman Rushdie and Amitav Ghosh among male writers, and its sexual and familial boundaries are ruptured by the thematization, for example, of homosexuality in Agha Shahid Ali's poetry, of bisexuality in Vikram Seth's poetry and fiction, and of lesbian identity and queer politics in Suniti Namjoshi's verse and prose.

Thirdly, many of the Indian-English writers in the diaspora occupy a remarkable spectrum of identities and backgrounds in relation to religion. Though broadly secular in content and perspective, the sheer diversity of the religious backgrounds of its authors—and hence also of their related ethnic, linguistic, regional and cultural origins on the subcontinent—constitutes one of the greatest strengths and source of fascination of this literature. We have several Muslim, Christian, Hindu and Parsi writers representing India in the diaspora.

Fourthly, the zone that has expanded the most in scope and effect in the diaspora is that of intercultural friendship and social relations that has proved vital for the maintenance of the Indian component in a culturally cosmopolitan identity. This division of cultural loyalties has contributed once again to the extensive revision of two key features of Indian writing in English. It has altered their conceptions of what constitutes their Indianness vis-à-vis the East-West encounter and done away with the earlier formulations offered by Kipling, Forster, and Raja Rao. Also, shifting away from the bookish Oxbridge norm of writing, the English language used by the Indian writers in the diaspora has moved towards a plethora of national, international, colloquial, generic and experimental styles. Finally, Indian immigrants and their descendants in different parts of the world differ from each other in their attitudes towards and actual connections with India, resulting in a corresponding spectrum of conceptions of India, Indian religions and cultures and especially of Indianness that is directly related to the psycho-social effects of displacement and dislocation. Though we are not certain what Indian English diasporic literature will look like ten years from now, we can safely conclude by stating that there will always be a new breed of writers whose origins are from this part of the decolonized world irrespective of which part of the world they are actually residing now.

Works Cited

Banerjee, Himani. *Thinking Through: Essays on Feminism, Marxism and Anti-Racism.* Toronto: Women's Press, 1995.

Barton, Laura. "A Passage from India." *The Guardian.* 15 December 2008.

Bhabha, Homi. *The Location of Culture*. London: Routledge, 1994.

Bhatia, Samita. "A Darker Vision." *The Telegraph* (Kolkata) 28 Jan. 2006.

Buford, Bill. "Declaration of Independence: Why Are There Suddenly so Many Indian Novelists?" *The New Yorker* (Special Fiction Issue), 23 & 30 June 1997. 6-7.

Carey, Gene. '"Ramji's Amrika": Interview with M.G. Vassanji.' *Rediff on the Net.* 15 December 2008.

Chaudhuri, Amit, ed. *The Picador Book of Modern Indian Literature.* London: Picador, 2001.

Clifford, James. "Further Inflections: Toward Ethnographies of the Future." *Cultural Anthropology*. 93 (3) (1994). 302-38.

Dawesar, Abha. "India Away From Home." *Indias Abroad: The Diaspora Writes Back*, ed. Pier Paolo Piciucco and Rajendra Patrick Chetty, Johannesburg: STE Publishers, 2004. 30-33.

Desai, Anita. "Modern Indian Writing: From the cave to a bazaar" *Graffiti, The Telegraph Magazine.* 2 Dec. 2007: 6-9.

—. "I Am Envious of Writers Who Are in India." (Interview with Nabanita Sircar), *India Today*. 30 October 2006. 82-83.

—. *The Inheritance of Loss*. New York: Atlantic Monthly Press, 2006.

Dharwadker, Vinay. "The Historical Formation of Indian English Literature." *Literary Cultures: Reconstructions from South Asia*, ed. Sheldon Pollock. Berkeley: U of California 2003. 199-267.

Ghosh, Amitav. "The Diaspora in Indian Culture." *The Imam and the Indian*, ed. Amitav Ghosh. Delhi: Permanent Black, 2002. 243-50.

Hall, Stuart. "Cultural, Identity and Diaspora." *Identity: Community, Culture, Difference*, ed. Jonathan Rutherford. London: Lawrence and Wishart, 1990. 223-37.

Kanaganayakam, Chelva. '"Broadening the Substrata": An Interview with M.G. Vassanji." *World Literature Written in English* 31.2, 1991. 19-35.

Khilnani, Sunil. (1997) *The Idea of India.* Rpt. New York: Penguin, 2003.

Lahiri, Jhumpa. 'Interview with Radhika S. Shankar: "Lahiri's First Book Gets Raves."' *Rediff on the Net.* 15 Dec. 2008.

Lal, Vinay. *The Other Indians: A Political and Cultural History of South Asians in America.* New Delhi: Harper Collins, 2008.

McLeod, Alan L., ed. *Literature of the Indian Diaspora: Essays in Criticism*. New Delhi: Sterling, 2000.

Martyris, Nina. "You Require Loneliness to Be a Writer." *The Times of India*. 10 Nov. 2008.

Mishra, Sudesh. "From Sugar to Masala: Writing by the Indian Diaspora." *An Illustrated History of Indian Writing in English,* ed. Arvind K. Mehrotra. Delhi: Permanent Black, 2003. 276-94.

Mukherjee, Bharati. *Darkness.* New York: Penguin, 1985.

Naipaul, Vidiadhar S. *A Writer's People: Ways of Looking and Feeling*. London: Picador, 2007.

Nelson, Emmanuel S., ed. *Writers of the Indian Diaspora: A Bio-Bibliographical Critical Sourcebook.* New York: Greenwood P. 1993.

Patel, Vibhuti. "Interview with Jhumpa Lahiri: "The Maladies of Belonging." *Newsweek International*. 15 Dec. 2008.

Prasannarajan, S. "Greed Killed Kashmir." *India Today*. 23 Sept. 2008.

Roy, Nilanjana S. "Write Society: Indo-Anglican Literature as a Doon School-St. Stephens Conspiracy." *India Today*. 7 February 2000. 69.

Rushdie, Salman. "Imaginary Homelands." *Imaginary Homelands: Essays and Criticism 1981-1991*. London: Granta, 1992. 9-21.

_____ and Elizabeth West, ed. *The Vintage Book of Indian Writing 1947-1997*. London: Random House, 1997.

Rushdie, Salman. *Shame*. London: Vintage Books, 1983.

Safran, William. "Diasporas in Modern Societies: Myths of Homeland and Return."*Diaspora* 1.1. 15 Dec. 2008.

Tlyan, K. "Rethinking Diaspora (s): Stateless power in the Transnational Moment." *Diaspora* 5: 3-35.

Vassanji, Moyez G. *The In-Between World of Vikram Lall.* London: Penguin Viking, 2003.

Tulsidom—the Physical and Cultural Setting in Naipaul's *A House for Mr. Biswas*: A Study

BIDHAN CHANDRA PAL

The themes of Naipaul's novels mostly revolve round the colonial psychosis, individual's search for identity and clash of culture. In A House for Mr. Biswas, *he deals with the theme of isolation, frustration and negation in a colonised society which turns cruel and callous to the aspiration of Mr. Biswas, the protagonist. The physical and cultural setting acquires a significant role in shaping the destiny and character of the individuals there. It is from this angle that Tulsidom in* A House for Mr. Biswas *forms the axis of the whole novel. The clash of cultures between the old and the new in a multiracial society is also one of the major themes of the novel. The hero represents all the Trinidad born Indians taking part in shaping of the diasporic existence by involving themselves in ethno-cultural issues. This article analyses the fate of men like Mr. Biswas living in a derelict land. Even his son Anand had the feeling of being led to inadequacies, lasting loneliness.*

V.S. Naipaul's *A House for Mr. Biswas* is a beautiful work which deals with the theme of isolation, frustration and negation in a colonised society—a society that turns cruel and callous to the aspirations of the protagonist, Mr. Mohan Biswas. The book also deals with a number of physical and spiritual maladies e.g. the clash of cultures between the old and the new in a multiracial society, a quest for identity in a conservative framework and above all, the protagonist's dry and monotonous journey, full of many jerks and jolts.

One of the ways through which Naipaul brings out isolation, frustration and negation in a colonised society is to invest the physical and cultural settings of his novels with symbolic or impressionistic significance. The setting in his novels is not merely a lifeless background against which human beings act and react; it is a potential means of shaping their destiny and character. In this connection I would like to cite the example of Thomas Hardy. In most of his Wessex novels, the country itself virtually becomes a character. This is particularly true of *The Return of the Native* in which Egdon Heath is a major force. Commenting on its role, Jean R. Brooks in an essay, "*The Return of the Native:* A Novel of Environment" writes:

> Egdon Heath, the resistant matter of the cosmos on which the action takes place, bears, shapes, nourishes and kills conscious organism possessed of its striving will without its unconsciousness of suffering. The six main characters take their key from Egdon. They all feel its pull through some affinity of temperament. Clym, Mrs. Yeobright and Diggory Venn share its look of isolation; Thomasin, Clym, and Venn its endurance; Eustacia and Wildeve, though they hate it, share its primal vitality and indifference to others. The rustics, too, take a more subdued tone from the heath. (21)

Even in *Tess of d'Urbervilles*, description of the places take on thematic or narrative significance, as well as providing a setting for the action of the plot. The two landscapes pose a series of contrasts: Summer versus Winter, a fertile paradise versus a barren wasteland, Angel Clare versus Alec d'Urbervilles. At Talbothays Dairy, Tess is a milkmaid whose daily ritual of work occurs in an environment of rich natural abundance and warmth. At Flintcomb Ash, she is a field hand, digging turnips from the frozen, unyielding earth in a setting dominated by the red threshing machine and the bleakness of the sky. In the earlier scene, Tess experiences the awakening of love for Angel Clare; in the later one, she undergoes a renewed threat from her seducer, Alec. In both cases the landscape serves as a projection of Tess's psychological state.

Indeed, Thomas Hardy and V.S. Naipaul as novelists are poles apart, whether in matters of theme, style and even temperament. Yet it cannot be denied that like Hardy, Naipaul has exhibited a rare skill in delineating the physical and cultural setting in his novels. The setting of Tulsidom in *A House for Mr. Biswas* is an example of exhibiting such a rare skill. The structure of the Tulsi establishment is very close to Ayemenem House in Arundhati Roy's *The God of Small Things*. In both the novels conservatism and patriarchal domination rule the roost. It is by making Mr. Mohan Biswas, the protagonist of *A House for Mr. Biswas*, rebel against the hypocrisies of the Tulsi family at Hanuman House that Naipaul lends an unusual complexity to his protagonist.

The encounter between Mr. Biswas and Mrs. Tulsi and Seth, the proprietary architects of the household, is described against the stark background of Hanuman House:

> Among the tumbledown timber- and corrugated-iron building in the High street of Arwacas, Hanuman House stood like an alien white fortress. The concrete walls looked as thick as they were, and when the narrow doors on the Tulsi store on the ground floor were closed, the house became bulky, impregnable and blank. The side walls were windowless and on the upper two floors the windows were mere slits in the facade. The balustrade which hedged the flat roof was crowned with a concrete statue of the monkey-god Hanuman. From the ground the white-washed features could scarcely be distinguished and were, if anything, slightly sinister, for dust had settled on projection and the effect was that of a face lit up from below. (80-81)

Such a description, indeed, seems to pass beyond naturalism into something symbolic or impressionistic. In an essay, "Assertion and withdrawal in Naipaul and Arun Joshi," Dr. C.N. Srinath shows the symbolic significance of Hanuman House:

> Hanuman House is a symbol of the conventional Hindu world with its superstitions, rituals, vagaries and hypocrisies. By making Mr. Biswas rebel against this world while simultaneously fighting the Tulsis who are out to curb his independence and crush his personality, Mr. Naipaul lends a complexity to his protagonist. Mr. Biswas is also the artist, the intellectual (in his own limited way) pitted against the Tulsi family which is materialistic enough to fit very well into the Hanuman House described above. They are insensitive to the creative aspect of their tradition to which they are supposed to belong but it is only the form, not the spirit of it that has come to have a sway on them. And as concrete evidence of this stands the mute, dusted statue of the monkey-god Hanuman at the entrance to the House. (63)

The stark atmosphere of the Hanuman House reminds me of *Wuthering Heights* of Emily Bronte where Heathcliff, like Mr. Biswas, has to undergo many undeserved miseries and sufferings. In chapter I of *Wuthering Heights* we have the following description:

> Wuthering Heights is the name of Mr. Heathcliff's dwelling, Wuthering being a significant provincial adjective, descriptive of the atmospheric tumult to which its station is exposed in stormy weather. It is set high up, the harsh, shelterless location eloquently expressed in the vegetation: one may guess the power of the North wind blowing over the edge, by the excessive slant of a few stunted firs at the end of the house; and by a range of gaunt thorns all stretching their limbs one way, as if craving alms of the sun. (4)

Lockwood's description of the house is stark: 'Deeply set in the wall, and the corners defended with large jutting stones.' We recall the furniture at Wuthering Heights includes chairs, 'One or two heavy black ones lurking in the shade,' and the background recedes vaguely into nightmare with 'other dogs haunted other recesses.' (5) it is clear that the weather and setting of *Wuthering Heights* are much more than an inanimate background. They are ambiguous, changeable extension of the characters' perceptions and moods, with a significance of their own woven into the text.

The development of the setting into an active element in the story is clearly palpable in Naipaul's *A House for Mr. Biswas.* The structure of the Tulsi establishment is viewed by Naipaul as the miniature form of the British colonial establishment where Mrs. Tulsi, the old queen and Seth are the coloniser and the husbands are the subjects. Mrs. Tulsi provides shelter and subsistence in return for total submission or abdication of self. It is a system which suppresses jealousy, individuality and superiority complexes. The Hanuman House with its leaders, its scheme of prescribed duties and responsibilities, its own law and order, religious rituals offer not only a coherent construction of the clan but reveals a slave society on closer examination.

It is this hypocrisy of the Tulsis and a gross contempt for man without money or position that antagonises Mr. Biswas. It is against this menacing, oppressive hold of the large household that Mr. Biswas revolts. He wants freedom and a personality. His relentless battle to achieve this is nullified by the Tulsi household at every stage. Hence acquiring a house becomes an obsession with Mr. Biswas, for that is the only way he can achieve freedom, both literally and otherwise from the Tulsis and gain a personality all his own.

In this connection it should be kept in mind that an important feature of Naipaul's fictional world is his delineation of the indentured Indian immigrants' dilemma. It depicts the exile's desire to strike root and attain an authentic selfhood in the fast-changing Caribbean world. There are parallels between the life of the author, the life of the protagonists and the fate of the sensitive and self-conscious colonial people. The author had to face many ups and downs in order to assert his identity in a disinherited tradition. He admits 'living in a borrowed culture, the West Indians, more than most, needs writers to tell him who he is and where he stands.' (*Middle Passage* 73) It is this cultural disinheritance that made Naipaul a great writer of Commonwealth literature. His anger, his frustration and futility, sprung from his sense of disinheritance. As a matter of fact, the secret of Naipaul's art lies not in his personal attachment to the establishment—individual, tradition, culture but in his creative detachment beyond geography, history and ethnicity.

In all novels of Naipaul, the characters have to undergo a lot of trials and tribulations, ups and downs. They long for a free and fair existence but unfortunately they are not able to cross the boundary of the colonial society. It is by making Mohan Biswas a rebel that Naipaul succeeds in turning his hero an archetypal figure, though we find him a wanderer. In Hanuman House, he is considered a buffoon playing the role of a fool. But Biswas, the clown, is also Biswas the rebel. The artistic aspect of his personality is real and this is what the Tulsis admire. When Biswas faces the meaningless void of life, he turns to his art as an anchor. Through his paint and brushes, he tries to create something against the emptiness. When Govind, one of the sons-in-law, asks him to give up sign-painting, Mr. Biswas is shocked: "Give up sign painting? And my independence? No, boy. My motto is: Paddle your own canoe." (107)

Sign-painting is Mr. Biswas's way of preserving his independence. His dream of the house is highly symbolic, which connotes stability and permanence, something solid in life. It represents also Mr. Biswas's partially successful attempt to escape from the ancient matriarchal order and medieval norms into a more western, private and candid state of life.

But the building of the house, however, is not an easy job. Mr. Biswas' several efforts to build a house according to his own choice falter. He is frustrated when he finds that he cannot grow a garden in spite of his best attempts. It is nothing but irony of circumstances that Mr. Biswas's new position poses certain new challenges which he is unable to face. He turns, ultimately, to the Hanuman House for security. When the house in Greenvale gets burnt, "An immense relief had come upon Mr. Biswas. The anxiety, the fear, the anguish which has kept his mind humming and his body taut now ebbed away. He could feel it ebbing; it was a physical sensation; it left him weak and very weary." (HB301)

Mr. Biswas's persistent desire to understand life and to assert his identity in a chastic world was thwarted. Persons like him cannot be allowed the luxury of stability and identity. It may be noted that he himself is not unaware of his ambivalent position. He tells his son: "I am just somebody. Nobody at all. I am just a man you know." (477). This is, obviously, the fate of men like Mr. Biswas, who are historically displaced and have the misfortune of living in a derelict land. Society offers very little possibilities to each one of them, and he has therefore no option but to balance his personal inadequacies against the contradictions of existence itself. (90)

N. Ramadevi says that Mr. Biswas has been inescapably trapped within his newly bought house. This indicates the failure and defeat implicit in every kind of fulfilment. It should be kept in mind that by the time Naipaul wrote the novel, he was convinced of the dark and unhopeful future of the former British colonies like Trinidad. Here he has narrated the gloom with dose of humour. He was looking at London as a land of promise. So at the end of *A House for Mr. Biswas*, escape from the area of darkness to outside has been suggested through the character of Anand. It appears that Mr. Biswas is not completely satisfied with his surroundings. So he starts living through Anand, his son, in London.

I cannot agree with Subir Dhar who feels that the novel is a record of a nation in the making. It is true that the novel shows gradually the traditional Hindu customs of the Tulsi clan get corroded to make space for the Creole culture of a nation in formation. In fact, in the novel we are shown that in the rituals of the Tulsis, the contradictions and ambiguities creep in. They chant incantation, worship idol in combination with crucifix and candle; celebrate Christmas in Creole style; consume Salmon fish on Friday. When somebody becomes ill, Hindu prayers, Indian and African superstitions and Western science are all called upon to contribute their remedies. They do registry marriage for the sake of convenience.

Their practices are sharply modified by the local environment. The problem of Mr. Biswas is his inability to belong either to Indian culture or to the new Caribbean culture. So he takes resort to Arya Samaj and finds scope to ridicule the Tulsis. Naipaul is, in fact, critical of the mythologized, claustrophobic orthodox Hindu world reconstructed in Trinidad.

Even in the context of the Indians' search for a meaningful place in the Creole world of Trinidad, though Biswas's shaky little house may signify journey's end, it equally suggests that their position remains uncertain and shadowed with anxieties. (Panwar 87) Anjali Gera in an essay, 'Strange Moves: Girmitya turns Cosmopolitan' points out: 'Naipaul emerges as the greatest problem, epitomising a particular diasporic ideology and transcending it. He is the mimic man who turns his master tools both against the master and his own people, the man without a home, the stranger, at home in a homeless Universe.' (Panwar 26)Actually Naipaul shows that a writer might be born in one nation, live in another and yet belong to another. It should be kept in mind that with the unique privilege of being a Diaspora, Naipaul has undergone all the problems of an exile. His vivid portrayals of life in the social and cultural milieu of Trinidad are painted from within. For Naipaul, the act of writing is not merely a matter of self-expression, but also an instrument of awareness seeking to modify social reality. Naipaul has dealt with how suffocated one feels when one is deprived of the basic existential needs like freedom, independence, identity and creativity.

There are controversies over Naipaul's depiction of the historical, political and creative potential of the Caribbean. But there is no controversy over his rare skill in creating a magnificent physical and cultural setting—the setting of Tulsidom in *A House for Mr. Biswas*. Through the setting, Naipaul has shown the predicament of Indian immigrants to the West Indies. Through the Tulsi establishment, he suggests that it is a half-made society with its mixture of cultures. The novelist is a member of this society which he denounces vehemently at times and he writes about it with an insider's knowledge. And it is the character of Mohan Biswas against his background, his revolt against the Tulsi establishment that imparts the striking success to the novel. Biswas's relationship with the Tulsi clan goes a long way in defining his struggle for selfhood. Tulsidom is a system that provides subsistence and shelter in return for total devotion and abdication of one's self. That's why Naipaul has depicted the Hanuman House as teeming with innumerable slaves subjected to inhuman bondage. The condition of these old men squatting on sacks on the ground and 'pulling at clay cheelums that glowed red and smelled of ganja and burnt sacking' (193) is really pathetic.

The glory of Tulsidom is its capacity to induce conformity among its members. Pitted against this, Mr. Biswas rebels in non-conformist acts and words and this is a significant step in his journey towards authentic selfhood. Like R.K. Narayan's Malgudi, where the Tamarind tree, the hill, the river Sarayu are inseparable with the life of Raju as the river lends poise to the convict Raju, the drought that makes him a near-martyr, the

Tulsi establishment in *A House for Mr. Biswas* paves the way for Mr. Biswas to struggle hard to free himself from the suffocating disintegrating, tradition ridden world. Indeed, the physical and cultural setting acquires a significant role in *A House for Mr. Biswas*.

Works Cited

Bala, Suman, ed. *V.S. Naipaul: A Literary Response to the Nobel Laureate*. New Delhi: Khosla, 2003.

Bronte, Emily. *Wuthering Heights*. New Delhi: Penguin, 1995.

Bloom, Harold, ed. *Wuthering Heights*. Bloom's Modern Critical Interpretations, 1987

Naipaul, V.S. *An Area of Darkness*. London: Penguin, 1964

_____. *A House for Mr. Biswas*. New Delhi: Penguin, 1992

_____. *The Middle Passage*. London: Andre Deutsch, 1962

Panwar, Purabi, ed. *V.S. Naipaul: An Anthology of Recent Criticism*. Delhi: Pencraft International, 2003.

Srinath, C.N. *The Literary Landscape*. Delhi: Mittal, 1986.

Glimpses on Partition: Interrogating Insanity and Religiosity: Sadat Hasan Manto's "Toba Tek Singh" and "Mozel"

OLIVIA SARKAR

The discussion mainly concerns with the experiences and sufferings of the common women and men consequent to partition whose feelings in very few instances have been given much importance. Rather they have been depicted as silent suffering hard. "Toba Tek Singh" is one of those few literary creations that depict individual common people vis-à-vis the massive mechanism of partition. Manto is even more interesting for few writers could treat partition with satire. The very concepts of religion and values have been satirically questioned through "Mozel": whether it is simply the rituals or love that builds Religion. Partition, a purely political affair is later worked out by the administration. Were the political leaders of the Hindus and the Muslims, who failed to see the consequences of the Partition, or were the British solely responsible for creating the catastrophic communal divide? Why the religion became the only determining factor in defining an individual during partition and all other identities of language, culture, and profession etc. got blurred? The political leaders took the decision of partition within the closed doors and considered it unnecessary to ask the masses their thoughts. The common people unless tutored by the politicians and their henchmen remained indifferent, at times apprehensive of the future. Sadat Hasan Manto depicted the picture of partition, its mechanicality, its apprehension and even the heartless bureaucratic enthusiasm that came at the weak of the event. He is probably unique in his recording of the common people's attitude and protest. Whether the decision of partition at the night before the dawn of independence is whimsical or the great, knowledgeable and experienced philosopher leaders got insane enough not to think of the aftermath of partition on the basis of religion lies under the big question mark. Even we, the so-called educated common mass never bothered to go into the truth of our respective religion and easily fall prey to the instigations of others. Every one of us suffers from a double identity. The strong Toba Tek Singh and the weak Tirlochen—now which one is insane and which is sane is open to question.

This paper comes out as a series of questions encircling the incident of Partition, which I believe, all of us have experienced directly or indirectly. A purely political affair, later worked out by administration, the tragedy of partition has been treated by historians in terms of figures and numbers and not at the level of human details. Only the authors tread the region beyond records. Partition literature poignantly captures the ravages of history on human hearts and lives: the unprecedented violence, uprooting, emotional scars, unresolved dilemmas and the colossal human waste. Sadat Hasan Manto went a step further and depicted the sufferings of a section of 'nonsense' lunatics whom nobody had ever cared for. Manto is even more interesting for his courage to put a blow on the face of those responsible for partition through his sharp satire.

A question often comes regarding justification of considering Manto as a writer on partition. There is no doubt that he is a leading one among the writers reflecting partition. His inclusion in any discussion of Indian literature is questioned on the ground of nationality. He was a Pakistani but he became so after the partition. Partition affected neither Indians nor Pakistanis. It affected the ill-fated dwellers of the subcontinent over whose hearts the partition line ran. Therefore, these writers on partition belong to a community common to both the countries. They are neither Indians nor Pakistanis. They are the affected people of the subcontinent.

There were several reasons for the birth of a separate Muslim homeland in the subcontinent, and all three parties—the British, the Congress and the Muslim League—were equally responsible. The British government had seen the Hindu Muslim unity during the revolt of 1857 and it grew apprehensive of the National Movement in which both the communities fought together for the country's freedom. The only way then to continue uninterrupted regime in India was to create a separation between the two communities. They followed the policy of "divide and rule." The British rulers created a rift between the Hindu Nationalists and the Muslim Nationalists to weaken the great Nationalist Movement. After 1872, they brought a shift in their policy towards the Muslims through appeasement of Muslims. They fanned religious sentiments of the Muslims and tried their best to sow the seeds of hatred and separation.

The British Government was also fearful of the potential threat from the Muslims, who were the former rulers of the subcontinent, ruling India for over 300years under the Mughal Empire. In order to win them over to their side, the British helped to establish the M.A.O. College at Aligarh and supported the All India Muslim Conference, both of which were institutions from which leaders of the Muslim League and the ideology of Pakistan emerged. As soon as the League was formed, they were placed on a separate electorate. "The leaders of the Muslim League fell an easy prey to the evil designs of the British rulers who were responsible for giving birth to the Muslim League in 1906 to counterpoise the rising nationalism. The implementation of the policy resulted in the Partition of Bengal in 1905, which was a move to create a permanent gulf between the two communities." (Chopra 14)

The British rulers were neither the true friend of the Muslims nor the foes of the Hindus; they were the truc friends of the British Imperialism and acted on the tested and tried maxim of *Divide et Impera.*" (Grover 604) First it suited the imperial interests to support the Hindus, so they supported them. "The early British economic and education policies looked upon the Muslims as chief conspirators in the revolt of 1857. They deliberately adopted the policy of suppressing the Muslims. As a punishment 27,000 Muslims were hanged to death in Delhi alone after the suppression of the revolt." (Chopra 14) Again when they noticed the exemplary unity between the communities, they extended the friendly hand towards the Muslims to check the tide of National Movement. On 14 January 1857, Lord Cross, State Secretary, wrote to Viceroy, Lord Duffrin, "The religious divide between the Hindus and the Muslims is very useful to us." (Majumder 322) They now sought to masquerade as the "champions" of the Muslims winning over the upper strata among them. (Bhardwaj 51). The Partition of Bengal along religious lines in 1905 was the first move to implement the policy of 'divide and rule.'

Moreover, immediately after the formation of Muslim League in 1906, the Morley Minto Reform Act, 1909, conferred upon the Muslims constitutional safeguards and weightage as a protection against the majority and "reward for the services rendered to the British Empire." The Government of India Act, 1935, provided separate electorates for Muslims and other communities. This was well known as 'communal award.' Under this award, the Muslims, the Europeans, the Sikhs, the Indian Christians, the Anglo-Indians and among the Hindus the depressed classed were to get separate electorates. (Sadashivam 61) It was the outcome of the elections fought under Government of India Act, 1935, in the years 1937 and 1946 that led eventually to the communalism, which became the cause of the birth of Pakistan.

The Hindu revivalists also deepened the chasm between the two nations. They resented the Muslims for their former rule over India. They rallied for a ban on the slaughter of cows, a cheap source of meat for the Muslims. They also wanted to change the official script from the Persian to the Hindu Devnagari script, effectively making Hindi rather than Urdu the main candidate for the national language. Congress also made several mistakes in their policies which further convinced the League that in an undivided India after Independence their interests will be totally suppressed. One such policy was the institution of "Bande Mataram," a national anthem which expressed anti-Muslim sentiments, in the schools of India where Muslim children were forced to sing it.

On the other hand, the religious fanatic forces led by the Muslim League demanded the Partition of India on the basis of the theory that the Muslims constituted a different nation from the Hindus. The leadership, concerned only with their own "narrow and selfish interests, raised the slogan of a separate Muslim state where they could have a free field for exploitation. So a separate state was a demand of hungry for power politicians, but generally Indians—Hindus and Muslims—took no interest in the proposed scheme and described it as impracticable.

The partition of India was not peaceful. It devastated both the countries. The violence it unleashed was unprecedented, unexpected and of course barbaric. Provoked by the hooligan actions of a few, the vengeance that the ordinary Hindus, Muslims and Sikhs wreaked on each other devastated our moral fabric, distorted our political judgment and deranged our understanding of moral rightness. The worst sufferers were the women since people of different communities punished one another by targeting their women by raping, dishonouring and abducting them.

The sensitive writers of India, Pakistan and Bangladesh captured the devastating impact of the Partition in its various aspects. Through this paper I am trying to reflect on the sharp satires of Sadat Hasan Manto in his two famous short stories "Toba Tek Singh" and "Mozel" to point out how craving for power made the once patriotic leaders insane enough to think of the partition of the country. But before going straightaway to that, let me resolve some basic questions related to partition.

What is a country? Is it the land occupied by a community of people later demarcated politically? Or is it the demarcated land in which people are later forced to stay? As we can understand the validity of the first answer, next comes the question of community and the basis of forming a community. A group of people forms a community when they can communicate with each other in a particular language i.e., communication is the basic factor.

It is the language which brings people nearer to form a group. One of the lunatics in the Lahore asylum placed a very interesting and crucial question: "Sardarji, why are we being sent to Hindustan? We can't even speak their language." (14) I think it is our own experience that we feel more comfortable with the people of Bangladesh than with a South Indian or a North Indian when the majority of them are Muslim. Perhaps we can communicate with them in our mother tongue which we can't in the case of the later ones. Even a lunatic was concerned about that. Then why religion became the only determining factor in defining an individual during partition and all other identities of language, culture, and profession got blurred?

A glimpse of the various countries and states of the world reveals that they are formed mostly on the basis of language. Even the Indian states are linguistically bordered. Then how the country has been split on the issue of religion? May be the leaders could not anticipate the global sensitive issue that will follow partition. This partition created a wide gulf between the Hindus and the Muslims throughout the globe not only of Hindustan and Pakistan. History is the evidence of largely peaceful co-existence between the two communities. Then how at the time of partition both became enemies? Did the political leaders of the Hindus and the Muslims became so power hungry that they failed to see the politics of the British behind this even after experiencing the partition of Bengal?

Was Partition only a British policy? The leaders took the decision of partition within the closed doors and considered it unnecessary to ask the masses their thoughts. Even the officers of the administrative machinery were over-enthusiastic to the farthest extreme. They had obvious reasons because for many it opened new vistas of upward mobility in career. The common people unless tutored by the politicians and their henchmen remained indifferent at times apprehensive of the future. Sadat Hasan Manto depicted the picture of partition, its mechanical approach, its apprehension and even the heartless bureaucratic enthusiasm that came at the peak of the event. He is probably unique in his recording of the common people's attitude and protest.

"Toba Tek Singh" is a poignant account of the irretrievable emotional loss caused by the partition. The story moves around Bishan Singh, a lunatic entrusted to the care of an asylum in Pakistan. He is also called Toba Tek Singh as he has large land holdings there. Once the partition is declared he, along with other non-Muslim lunatics, is forced to migrate to India as both the governments have decided to transfer the lunatics along with other people. Though he is mad, Bishan Singh loves his land dearly. The thought of leaving his land gives him immense pain. Before he is forced to migrate to India he wants to know whether Toba Tek Singh is in India or in Pakistan. When he comes to know that it is in Pakistan he becomes very sad. He is not ready to leave his own country. When the evacuation process is going on he refuses to enter the other country. He remains standing in the place where he stands while transfer of other lunatics continues. At the end before sunrise he falls sick and lies prostrate on the ground prostrate. Beyond a weird fence on one side of him was Hindustan and on the other side was Pakistan. In the middle on a stretch of land which has no name, lies Toba Tek Singh. He dies in the no man's land.

Bishan Singh is the representative of millions of people on both sides of the borders who never wanted to leave their homeland but were forced to forsake their land due to the whims of the power monger leaders. Even the lunatics intensely feel the sense of loss. They have nothing to do with the materialistic pursuits since they are mad. They too have feelings and love for land and the bonds they have enjoyed with their fellow human beings. They cursed all the leaders both Muslims and Hindus, who were responsible for splitting Hindustan into two.

The story compels us to ask: Are the inmates really mad? Let's see what they say:

> What is Pakistan?—A place in India where they manufacture razors. (14)

Symbolically, it may be the sharp weapon that apparently cut human heads and profoundly cut human minds during riots to create Pakistan.

Not only Bishan Singh but other lunatics like him were also sad at heart when they were told about the transfer. One of them a Muslim, first climbed on a tree and when threatened by the guards he said, "I want to live neither in Pakistan nor in Hindustan. I will live on this tree." (15) "When he comes down, he embraces his Hindu and Sikh friends and cries bitterly and is saddened by the thought of their impending departure to India." (15) India or Pakistan was irrelevant to them in relation to their native village. Gradually, the location of Toba Tek Singh posed a very crucial question: "Who could guarantee that both Pakistan and Hindustan would not disappear someday?" (16)

Two lunatics declared themselves as Mohammad Ali Jinnah and Tara Singh respectively. The authorities apprehending the danger confined them in separate quarters. But India could not confine the power hungry leaders of the Congress or the Muslim League who fell easy prey to the evil designs of the British rulers. The 'sane' India could not understand that the rioters are never friends to anybody. They spread communalism only for their vested interest.

The protagonist Bishan Singh though mad knew the importance of love and human relationship. He may have to stay in the asylums throughout his life which do not differ in India or Pakistan. Still he does not want to leave his land. He could perhaps feel himself honoured to stay in his own country. When he asks one of the lunatics who believes himself to be 'God' about the location of Toba Tek Singh, he replies, "It is neither in Pakistan nor in Hindustan, because I have not given any orders yet." (17) He is like the whimsical persons who do not know their country and its people properly but started thinking that everything will happen as they wish and order. There are also the representatives of a section of common masses who without knowing anything starts shouting "Pakistan Zindabad!" "Pakistan Murdabad." (18) They are the most dangerous.

Lastly, when Bishan Singh knew that Toba Tek Singh is in Pakistan he became adamant, unwilling to leave his motherland. Everyone tried to convince him. The guards could not befool him by telling lies that if he's (Toba Tek Singh, the village) not there yet, they will send him there immediately. (18) When the British fooled the sane population by the false talk of resolving all problems through partition, can Bishan Singh be called a lunatic?

Bishan Singh is the symbol of honour and love for one's motherland. When the great country India had been scandalized by riots, murders, abduction and rapes, the small insignificant Toba Tek Singh attained the highest place of honour through his death. Can he be called a lunatic in the true sense of the term?

The author also gives him an honourable position. In the whole story when all others called him Toba Tek Singh out of humour, the author retained his name as if to identify the distinguished person who did not surrender himself to the tide of temporary fanaticism. On the other hand in the last paragraph the author addressed the dead body of Bishan Singh as Toba Tek Singh to personify the homeland of Bishan Singh. He could not know where his Toba Tek Singh lies, in Pakistan or in Hindustan. So he died in the no man's land, in neither of the countries. His usual gibberish, "Oper di gur gur di annexe di bay dhania di mung di daal" (18) which changes time to time is a symbolic expression of disgust to show how non-sensical the idea of partition is.

In "Mozel," Manto launched scathing attacks on ritual-oriented religion. He voiced through the Jewish girl, Mozel who apparently a callous, irresponsible, valueless girl questioned the very concepts of religion, duty, honesty and above all love when time came. Tirlochen, a Sikh guy loved her deeply and wanted to marry her but she always refused on the ground that "You're a Sikh." (115) On her demand, he even shaved off his beard and got his hair cut but still could not marry her because of her callous, irresponsible nature. Superficially, it may appear that Mozel is superstitious about religion, but her naked dead body overturned the entire idea. She did not hate a Sikh but a coward, who had neither true respect for his religion nor courage to break the showy religious rituals. He slept with a number of girls and tried the same with Mozel but when he was asked to save his fiancée Kirpal, he could not go in front of her without his turban, though inside it there were no 'kesh.'

On the other hand, Mozel flirted with so many men, but never allowed them to cross the limit of her chastity, not even Tirlochen. Because of her callous dressing once Tirlochen warned her of modesty which irritated her and she asked, "If you're so conscious of it, why don't you close your eyes? You're an adult and you still believe that your religion is in your underwear." (118)

Tirlochen also after shaving off his beard and cutting off his kesh felt with certainty that he had been carrying a burden that really had no meaning. Tirloch's religiosity reached its extreme nonsense when he wanted to put on his turban in spite of the dangers it could bring to him and Kirpal. If the Muslim riots killed them because of being Sikhs, then for whom the ritual? Religion made him blind and he could not understand the simple truth.

But Mozel, like a brave lover, courageously guided him among the police and the rioters. To save Tirlochen and Kirpal, she did not have a second thought to undress herself and put it over Kirpal so that the Muslims could not recognize her. She did not care for her chastity which she saved from even the person she loved. Rushing naked in front of the rioters, its result we can easily understand. But at that moment there was no way out. She slipped from the stairs and was wounded mortally. She was about to die when Tirlochen removed his turban and covered her body. Perhaps the true form of religion stripped off all rituals is revealed at this critical moment.

But Mozel pushed the turban away from her body and said, "Take away . . . this religion of yours" (127) Tirlochen is the representative of the common masses who out of cowardice could not challenge the false rituals of religion when the human race is at stake. Manto perhaps intended to place the big question: Have men created religion or religion created mankind? The common masses do not like riots to happen but they also cannot protest.

Who is truly religious—Tirlochen or Mozel—one who maintained the show or the one who, in spite of all apparent valuelessness, understood the depth of it? Manto questioned the very concepts of religion and values satirically through Mozel: whether it is simply the rituals or love that builds religion. What should be the first and foremost religion of a human being—love for humanity or hatred towards his fellow siblings? The Muslim lunatic and the flirt girl felt the truth. But we, the so-called educated common masses never bothered to go into the truth of our respective religion and easily fell prey to the instigations of others. Every one of us possesses the double identity: the strong Toba Tek Singh and weak Tirlochen. Now which one is sane and which insane is open to question.

Whether the decision of partition at the night before the dawn of independence is whimsical or great, knowledgeable and experienced leaders and philosophers got tired and insane enough to continue the national movement and preferred a "safer route" to power. Whether it is justified or not is a thousand dollar question. Years later, a British author, Leonard Mosley, recounted a conversation with Nehru that rings true. The Prime Minister told him in 1960: "The truth is that we were tired men, and we were getting on in years too. Few of us could stand the prospect of going to prison again and if we had stood out for a united India as we wished it, prison obviously awaited us. We saw fires burning in the Punjab and heard every day of killings. The plan for Partition offered a way out and we took it." (Chopra xxv-xxvi)

What the leaders could not do, Bishan Singh does. He holds his ground, his motherland till death. In course of describing the inmates of the Lahore asylum, Manto confused our understanding of the fine line between sane and insane. As he progresses the line gets thinner and ultimately wipes out. Who is sane and who insane? The sane India is the Lahore asylum or the Lahore asylum is sane India. Manto's subtle satire slapped the idea of so-called 'sane.'

There is or was a Toba Tek Singh in all of us but being a so-called sane (or insane?) man we could not hold our ground till death like the mad (or wise?) fellow.

Works Cited

Chopra, Vinod K. *Partition Stories: Mapping Community, Communalism and Gender*. New Delhi: Anamika, 2009.

Grover, B.L. and Grover, S. *A New Look at Modern Indian History* .New Delhi: S. Chand, 2000.

Majumder, R.C. , ed. *The British Paramountcy and Indian Renaissance*, Part X. Mumbai: Bharatiya Vidya Bhawan, 1982.

Manto, Sadat Hasan. "Toba Tek Singh" and "Mozel" in Frank Stewart and Sukrita Paul Kumar, ed. *Crossing Over*. Manoa: University of Hawaii Press, 1991.

Sadasivam, S.N. *Party and Democracy in India.* New Delhi: Tata McGraw Hill, 1977.

"Recovering for Whose Sake": Studying Abduction and Recovery in the Context of Partition in Rajinder Singh Bedi's "Lajwanti"

SOMDEV BANIK

Partition fiction from the Western front is replete with characters unwilling to migrate from their place of birth or such who question the idea of partitioning the subcontinent. Yet whenever such characters were women, they were either left behind by their own family, or abducted and married off or raped and let off by their own neighbours or sold off to slavery in Afghanistan. There were thousands of such women rendered destitute by the partition. Post-independence, the governments of either country passed Bills to recover such 'abducted' *women from their places of origin and bring them to their new nations. This act of recovery to undo the initial act of violence was in fact counterproductive, as it rendered the women even further vulnerable in the new country. This paper proposes to study the facets of partition violence on women by taking up Rajinder Singh Bedi's Urdu story "Lajwanti". In the process, it deconstructs the myth of Lajwanti, the flower and raises the issue of double dispossession of women in the act of Independence. It also attempts to analyse the necessity of the nations to recover its 'abducted' subject citizens from the hands of the enemy.*

The great Indian Independence and Partition were two sides of the same coin, yet the euphoria of Independence subsumed the pangs of Partition and relegated the narratives of disruption, dislocation and ruthless violence to the deep chasms of forgetfulness. Though for majority of Indians, Independence signified liberation from colonial rule, for the two states of Punjab and Bengal, the *azadi* was one of bewildering loss: of place and property, community, of stable relationships and of a coherent identity. Over eight million people crossed the newly created borders of these states while half a million lost their lives in widespread communal violence. As it happens, the cost of Partition had to be borne mostly by women and children, the two most vulnerable sections of mankind. In fact, as Jisha Menon has noted, "the violence between Hindus, Muslims and Sikhs was enacted upon the bodies of the women of all three communities" (30). As women were considered embodiments of the sanctified, inner recesses of culture and tradition, they too easily became real targets of violent assertions of not only the 'other' community and nation but also of their own. More than 50000 Muslim women in India and 33000 Hindu and Sikh women in Pakistan were abducted since 1 March 1947 to 1 January 1949. This abduction of women was viewed quite seriously by the state of India, which passed the Abducted Persons' Bill on 31 December 1949 to recover those women, abducted and forcibly converted by the 'enemy' and restore them to their respective families and countries where they were presumed to rightfully belong. This recovery mission continued up to 1956, for almost a decade; in the mean time however many abducted women had settled down by marrying their abductors or anyone else from the other community. Recovering from the loss of their near ones, they resigned to their fate and carried on with life. The Recovery Mission displaced many such women once more while repatriating them to their families. While restoring them, it completely overruled their choice in the matter and the police officers in charge of the recovery were given virtually unlimited powers and complete immunity from enquiry and action. Not so of course for thousands of Muslim men who decided to stay back and accepted citizenship of India. The question now is why did the Government of India go to such extent only to recover the so-called abducted women when a huge number of Muslim men stayed behind? Was it out of a humanitarian concern or was there something more at stake? The question is pertinent, for many women who were reclaimed simply refused to return to their homes, preferring the anonymity and relative autonomy of the ashrams to a now alien family (Menon and Bhasin, 6). My contention in this paper is that if abduction was an act of criminal violence against those women, their forcible recovery by the state after several years was equally a violent affront on them. Though enacted in the name of dignity, it forced them to a life of destitution and marginalization for the rest of their lives. And this can't be better illustrated than through the travails of one such woman, Lajwanti, in Rajinder Singh Bedi's Urdu short story of the same title translated in English by Alok Bhalla (Ramakrishnan 2005).

Sunderlal migrated during Partition from Pakistan leaving behind his wife Lajwanti who had been abducted. Post-independence, efforts were carried out under the supervision of Miss Mridula Sarabhai, a high profile social worker, to recover thousands of such women from West Punjab, now in Pakistan. In Mohalla Shakoor, where Sunderlal had settled down, a committee was formed to help rehabilitate such women in their families, with Sunderlal as the secretary. Every morning and evening processions were taken out stressing the innocence and haplessness of recovered women and urging their reluctant, sceptical families to accept them. Sunderlal missed his beautiful wife and fondly remembered those days in village with her. He regretted those days when he had beaten her for every trifle and marvelled at her resilience. He

> would feel tormented by memories of his wife and he would swear to himself, "if I ever find her again, if I ever again do . . . I shall honour her and give her a place in my heart. . . . I shall tell everyone that the women who were abducted are innocent. They are victims of the brutality and the rapacity of the rioters. . . . A society which refuses to accept them back, which does not rehabilitate

> them . . . is a rotten, a foul society, which should be destroyed. (519)

As a responsible, considerate citizen, Sunderlal would exhort people, "Never remind them, either by word or gesture of the humiliations they have suffered; don't ever reopen their wounds. They are gentle and fragile like the leaves of the Lajwanti . . . if you touch them they will curl up and die" (519). One day Lajwanti returned. She was in a red dupatta worn in a typical Muslim fashion; Sunderlal was very excited to see her and at the same time 'shocked.'

> Lajo looked healthier than before, her complexion looked clearer, her eyes brighter and she had put on weight. She looked different from what he had *imagined* (my italics). He had thought that suffering and sorrow would have reduced her to a mere skeleton. . . . He was startled to see that she had been well treated in Pakistan. He was puzzled. "If she had been comfortable and happy there, why did she agree to return?" he wondered. (526-27)

For Sunderlal it was "strangely disturbing. But he did not flinch from doing his *duty*, and behaved in a manly and courageous manner" (527). Sunderlal, unlike those who refused to accept their recovered women, magnanimously "*enshrined Lajo like a golden idol in the temple of his heart and guarded her like a jealous devotee*" (528). Henceforth, he addressed her as 'Devi,' thus disembodying her of her womanhood. Lajo, on the other hand, was happy to be back. But she wanted to tell Sunderlal of all she had suffered, her ignominies and violations, but he refused to listen to her 'sinful' past. Lajo wanted to be her old self again, redeem her right as Sunderlal's wife. Slowly though she realized that the Partition had enacted an irreversible split within herself, and she has lost her body for ever. If Sunderlal has accepted her it is minus her body, and she has to live a disembodied existence for the rest of her life.

As a short story, "Lajwanti" is marked by overt authorial intrusion, justifiably quite so, as Rajinder Singh Bedi was dealing with a very sensitive national issue. Sunderlal is the only fully drawn character engaged in a social campaign against the conservative sections of the society represented by the priests of Narain baba's temple. Through this story the author wanted to uphold the issue that was raging both inside and outside parliament, during the first decade of independence. Naturally, the protagonist Babu Sunderlal represents the nationalist, secular, progressive point of view as against the conservative, communal and patriarchal zealots for whom conversion and cohabitation with someone other than the husband deserved nothing less than death. It is worth pointing out here that even Gandhi and Nehru had issued public appeals in 1946 and 1948 to take back such girls and women and give them respect and honour. Interestingly, in this debate between the nationalists and the conservatives, the women were conspicuously left out without any voice or choice. It was presumed that all abducted women held captive by the 'enemy' nation wanted nothing more than to return to their original families, as soon as possible. Such generalized supposition by the state and the community on behalf of adult citizens problematizes this issue and exposes its patriarchal bias.

How was an abducted person defined? An abducted male must be below 18 years; though a woman can be of any age, separated from his or her family and is found to be living with or under the control of any other individual or family, between 1 March 1947 and 1 January 1949. An 'abducted person' in case of a woman refers to the one who had stayed behind in the place where she was born and grown up, whereas her family was forced out to a new nation. The new nation on the basis of filed complaint by the family appropriates the authority to reclaim that 'abducted' woman from the newly defined 'enemy territory.' The state thus becomes the new parent patriarch, assuming the moral responsibility on behalf of the failed father/brother/son to relocate and restore the subject within her family, community and country, even though after a good, many years.

Why women and girls were targeted for abduction, rape/ murder and conversion by the members of the other community in such huge numbers? Concurrently, why were so many women urged to take their lives and be martyrs by their own families and community? And then why was it again so crucial for the new nation to reclaim those 'polluted' women and reinstate them to their original families? Traditionally women are invested with inviolate sanctified values of a community by the patriarchy and are expected to protect those values from defilement. A woman is thus the signifier of the purest and most sanctified essence of a community and nation. Defiling and converting a woman thus acquire a political and symbolical significance, that of corrupting the core of the community. It also signifies humiliation and emasculation of the men folk of that community, and thereby assertion of identity of the aggressor. At the same time, to prevent abduction and conversion women are often urged to take their own lives, or are killed by their own families for protecting honour and purity. Thus the woman's body becomes the site on which the fight for honour and identity of both communities is worked out. It is also for the very same reason that there is so much reluctance in accepting a polluted woman back in her family. Because that woman not only is rendered 'sexually impure' but is a persisting reminder of the failure and humiliation of the patriarchal family and the patriarchal community. Patriarchy shifts the responsibility of its failure back to the woman by expecting her to choose death over loss of honour. "Why didn't they die? Why didn't they take poison to preserve their virtue and honour. . . . Cowards, clinging to life!" (520) Survival after abduction and conversion is regarded as unethical and unacceptable by the family and community.

Why did the state of India undertake this Recovery Operation then, if there was so much reluctance at the family and community level? Even though India is a self-defined secular nation, partition was implicitly worked out on the basis of two religions. Hence, identity and citizenship of those women who were left behind by their families were defined in terms of religion and community and forced to return to the Muslim nation created for the Muslims. This was irrespective of the fact that these women were born and living in India till Partition like other Hindus. This points to certain disjunction between the state's professed secular rhetoric and the communal identification of the 'abducted' women. Moreover, the Recovery Operation, as pointed out by Ritu Menon and Kamla Bhasin, was 'articulated and implemented within the parameters of two overriding factors: first, the relationship of the Indian state with Pakistan and second, its assumption of the role of 'parens patriae' *vis-à-vis* the women who had been abducted. As the former, it was obliged, as a "responsible and civilized" government of a civilized country to rightfully claim its subject-citizens as the latter was morally bound to relocate and restore these same subjects within their family, community and country. This dual role and responsibility simultaneously cast Pakistan itself as the abductor-country and India as the parent-protector, safeguarding not only her women but, by extension, the inviolate family, the sanctity of the community, and ultimately the integrity of the whole nation. Additionally, and recurrently, the moral, political and ideological importance of India's secularism was held up as an ideal that had to be vigorously championed and defended (Menon and Bhasin: 8). Even for Mridula Sarabhai, the chief social worker of the Operation, the recovery work was not only a humanitarian problem; it was a part of her political ideology. It was the social responsibility of the state, she believed, to restore its subject citizens to the place where they legitimately belonged to and which only will entitle them to a life of 'izzat.' It was assumed that no woman could be happy with her abductor husband or in the abductor country, and wanted nothing more than to be restored to her original family. A union between a Hindu/Sikh woman and a Muslim man could not be accepted as it transgressed both the norms of traditional marriage and religion. A child born of such a union would be forever illegitimate. Being the father patriarch, the state couldn't have allowed such transgression and violation of the most critical site of patriarchal control—the woman's sexuality. So those women needed to be restored from any 'illegal arrangement' with the religious other to a legitimate family, one that is sanctioned by the community and the nation. A woman's choice obviously couldn't be allowed to act as a factor in this project of upholding national and communal honour.

Recovery was then a symbolically significant activity undertaken by the patriarchal nation on behalf of the patriarchal family and community to restore and convert back the abducted woman into the Hindu fold. The families had to be persuaded to overcome their shame and reluctance through public appeals, propaganda work and distribution of pamphlets. Analogies were drawn with the abduction of Sita, who in spite of being in Ravana's custody was as pure as ever. Manusamhita was quoted, to convince that a woman having sexual intercourse with anyone other than her husband, becomes purified after three menstrual cycles and hence her family could accept her back (Butalia 18). Gandhi and Nehru stressed again and again on innocence, purity and fragility of these women while urging the families to take them back. Gandhiji said in 1946, "if anyone of those recovered women should come to me, then I will give them as much respect and honour as I accord to these young maidens." (Butalia 7). Nehru appealed through newspapers in 1948, "these girls and women require our tender and loving care and their relatives should be proud to take them back and give them every help" (Butalia 7). So the state and the community consistently projected the innocent victimhood of the women, thereby divesting them of any agency. As the patriarchal forces were fixated with the violation of their sexuality, the ordeal faced by the women was one of defeat, shame and dishonour. On the other hand, if the violated women had committed suicides to protect their honour, these women would have been glorified and called martyrs. There was no glory considered in their survival and suffering, and the past be better buried in mortifying silence. As one survivor had even refused to recall those days saying, "Dafa karo, hun ki yaad karna hai. Dafa karo (Bury it. What's the point in recalling the past? Forget it)" (Butalia 6). She was just echoing the sentiments of the patriarchal society, for accepting its verdict at the cost of silencing her past.

All these had contributed to the construction of the recovered woman's identity and the patriarchal society's attitude towards her. Babu Sunderlal's attitude to Lajwanti was no exception. Even the trope of the touch-me-not flower reinforced this construction:

> Do not touch Lajwanti
> For she will curl up
> and die. (517)

Interestingly, Rajinder Bedi, in using this trope has downplayed two other characteristics of this same flower. Lajwanti is also a thorny plant and irrespective of its curling up, it does not die so easily. Touch-me-not is a unique survivor. In fact, both these characteristics redeem Lajwanti (the flower) from a passive victimhood to an agency, where it can not only protect itself, but also survive all onslaughts. The construction of Lajwanti (the character) as an innocent, passive, fragile victim of violence in need of male protection and care perpetuates her sense of victimhood. The patriarchal family/community accepts the sexually violated woman (Lajwanti, in this case) in its own terms and not as the same woman of before. It splits her past from her present and suppresses the painful past behind a pall of silence, under the pretext that the only way of dealing with the painful past is through suppression and erasure of the memory. As Sunderlal urges people, "Never remind them, either by word or gesture, of the humiliations they have suffered; don't ever reopen their wounds. They are gentle and fragile like the leaves of the lajwanti" (519).

Secondly, patriarchal society enacts a split between the recovered woman's body and soul. The body which was violated is banished and made invisible and the woman is accepted as a disembodied self. Even though she is accepted back, she loses her conjugal rights, and is reincarnated as Devi, reborn on the sacrificial pyre of her body. Lajo, thus could never be the same Lajo again, her body lost forever on the altar of partition.

But like every other recovered woman, Lajo also wanted to tell Sunderlal, "all that she had suffered so that she could feel clean again" (528). But she was silenced every time, by the strange look in Sunderlal's eyes. It is crucial that Lajo and other women like her defying patriarchy tell their story to others. The act of narration only would reinstate such victims to the position of subjecthood, and their survival itself then would be heroic achievements, not acts of shame and dishonour as patriarchy would have them believe. It's only through narrating and sharing and not through erasure, that Lajo could reclaim her identity and be her true self once again.

Works Cited

Bhalla, A. "Lajwanti" *Indian Short Stories, 1900-2000*, ed. E.V. Ramakrishnan. Delhi: Sahitya Akademi, 2005.

Butalia, U. "Community, State and Gender: On Women's Agency during Partition," *EPW*, Vol. 28, No. 17 (1993): 12-21.

Menon, R & Bhasin, K. "Recovery, Rupture, Resistance: Indian State and Abduction of Women during Partition." *EPW*, Vol. 28, No. 17 (1993): 2-11.

Menon, J. "Rehearsing the Partition: Gendered Violence in 'Aur Kitne Tukde Feminist Review," *Postcolonial Theatres*, Vol. 84 (2006): 29-47.

Partition: A Metaphor of Mourning, Memory and Identity Crisis—Flashed in the Pages of Post-Independence Indian English Fiction

NIRMALYA BHATTACHARYYA

Partition of colonial India created two nations, India & Pakistan, keeping the human values and identity of the people at stake. The "refugee special" trains then marked the history of these two nations. Eternal human values were supplemented by cruel communal feelings and religious identity that overpowered all other ways of being and relating to each other. In the midst of this unspeakable horror, the Indian English writers of the post-independence period reflected the dark shadows of partition that had been cast on thousands of innocent faces. Due to its relative distance from other Indian languages as well as its circumscribed readership, the Indian English fiction seems to have been able to undertake a more sustained engagement with the ugliness and pain of that moment in a historical frame. Considering all these facts this paper will focus on some post-Independence Indian English fiction that undertook the task of naming and describing that fratricidal violence. The paper will bring out the glimpses of the partition and its impact on the lives of the people of the both sides of the border as portrayed by Khushwant Singh, Salman Rushdie, Amitav Ghosh and other post-Independence Indian English fiction writers.

Partition in the Indian sub-continent created such a history for both India and Pakistan, which is unforgettable for many reasons. Whether the decision of partition and creating two countries was right or wrong is a debatable issue but no one can debate with the fact that this partition caused a devastating violence and a painful memory so much fresh that the people of these two countries are still carrying the burden of it. The partition of India was the result of several years of political planning or a strong game plan between the-then leaders of the Indian National Congress, the Muslim league and the British Government (Hasan 63). This political scheming of partition resulted in a bloodbath on both sides of the border which shattered all human values. Partition resulted in communal riots as over ten millions of people—Sikhs, Hindus, and Muslims—were dislocated from their homes and became refugees. At least a million were killed in retaliatory violence undertaken by members of all three communities while thousands of women were abducted, raped, and in many instances, forced to commit suicide to preserve the 'honour' of their communities (Gopal 69). Although the enormous loss of property, the number of persons beaten, injured, tortured, raped, abducted and otherwise physically assaulted can be measured, the emotional pain of partition from home, family and friends is obviously immeasurable and more tormenting than the physical trauma. Thus, no citizen of Indian and Pakistan having a sense of history and living in this post-colonial or post-independence era can ignore the impact of partition on contemporary life. It is quite obvious that the Partition is not only a historical fact; its implications are much more, as it becomes a theme for many of the writers of the Indian subcontinent continuously influencing the literary activities of Indian sub-continent. The cruelties and the horror made the affected dumbstruck, so much so that many of them did not dare to recall their horror-stricken days. The writers have taken up the task to break the silence and to portray the grim phase of this partition in their literary pieces. The communal riot, disarray of human life and the overall consequences of the partition is a vital theme of the many post-independence Indian English fiction. Novels which are significant in bringing out the glimpses of partition and will form the subject matter of this paper are: Khushwant

Singh's *Train to Pakistan* (1956), Salman Rushdie's *Midnight's Children* (1980) and Amitav Ghosh's *The Shadow Lines* (1988).

Partition-effect being a vital issue has always been a subject matter for various writers of the subcontinent. Some of the earlier writings about partition predominantly written in Hindi, Urdu and other Indian local languages focus much on scenes of bloodshed to evoke a feeling of disgust in the reader; these seem to portray the demented hatred between the Hindus and the Muslims at that time in India. There were also other writings, which are strictly free from any communal bias. This is amply evident from Saadat Hasan Manto's slim volume of sketches called *Siyah Hashye* published soon after the partition. Manto can be identified as a unique presenter of the partition theme. In his writing, Manto, except for one instance, has never given any religious identity to any of his characters involved in the brutal killings. But it is not Manto alone who has tried to deviate from the contemporary style of representation of the partition-theme; there are others too applying some different voices and different techniques to portray this theme and its impact in their pieces. Meenakshi Mukherjee is quite justified to say that the theme of Partition has a 'pervasive' impact on the Indian bhasha literatures (180). The same is also true in the context of Indian English Novel writing. Though in the 1930s, the Indian English fiction flourished but like other novels written in vernacular languages, it also concentrated on consolidating the idea of nation and its identity (Mukherjee 173). After independence, the aftermath of partition was so immense in the psyche of the people of both the nations that it had a long term influence in the socio-political, economic and literary activities. Therefore, the theme of partition among the Indian English Fiction writers gradually became an experience that explores and conceives the social, political, religious and cultural intricacies of the Indian subcontinent.

Khushwant Singh's *Train to Pakistan* (1956)
A Historical Account of Human Tragedy

Train to Pakistan by Khushwant Singh was the first Indian English novel to put forth partition as a theme. Khushwant Singh himself was the victim of the partition as he had to leave his beloved city Lahore and had to land in Delhi, like hundreds and thousands of people. The account of partition by Khushwant Singh in *Train to Pakistan* was his own experience; the same being experienced by the entire sub-continent. Stanley Wolpert, one of the reputed historians of the partition of Indian sub-continent acknowledges the intellectual ability of Khushwant Singh by saying that Khushwant Singh's novel Mano Majra (*Train to Pakistan*) had first made him aware of the human impact of Partition's tragedy on Punjab' (18). In fact, this novel is unique as it reflects both the yearning of a victim and as well as the inner cries of a writer.

The novel *Train to Pakistan* is about a sleepy village, Mano Majra on the border of India and Pakistan. Being situated by the side of railway track, Mano Majra as a village is very much conscious of the movements of trains, trains that epitomize the brutality of Indo-Pak partition. As during the period of partition, over ten million men and women were forced to flee on either side of the borders and as trains were the means to carry people from one side of the border to another side, it was selected for human slaughter. Trains crammed with refugees headed across the newly demarcated borders were stopped and their passengers were butchered before the train was allowed to cross the border. Mano Majra is also affected by the passing of the trains as these broke the calmness of the village. Now 'ghost trains' passing at odd hours are disturbing the dreams of the village. The novel depicts the horrible picture of a day when a train carrying the passengers stops by the village and later on when the flames of mass cremation whirled into the sky of the dark night. Amidst the silence of eternal death and the odour of the burning dead bodies, the villagers realized that their fate is no more in their hands; it has already been decided by the political leaders.

The novel becomes more interesting when it tries to account for the ways in which neighbours become 'others' and 'murderers.' Stirring the mild-mannered peasants of Mano Majra to violence proves to be a daunting task for the outsiders and organized criminals who come in to undertake it. What the ordinary folks of Mano Majra cannot grasp is precisely the history-altering dimensions of what has taken place. The irony of the whole thing lies in the fact that the people of this village will not only be a part of this history of carnage, they will also have to participate in it as representatives of homogenized communities rather than as individuals. What Singh points out here is that only death and brutality will characterize the faith of these two newly created nations. Significantly enough, the trains running to and fro Mano Majra are shown by Singh to regulate the life of the village and its inhabitants. Thus, the disruption in the railway schedule after the partition serves in the novel as a sign of social chaos. This anarchy points out only to the helplessness of human beings amidst the political and social changes. When the hopes of the Muslims of Mano Majra leave their native land forever, the reader notices that destiny does not play any role to determine the fate of these hapless people but the rulers or politicians. Bereft of all their hopes, they begin to realize that they are too feeble to stop losing everything, and yet are powerless to do anything about this. It is unique the way this ironic building up of loss is dramatized in the novel, showing the utter helplessness of common men under the influence of irrepressible demonic forces. The chapter in which this happens is both very crucial and a representative one in the novel, as the incidents that took place in this village were actually happening both in Punjab and Bengal in 1947.

Train to Pakistan is not a sketch of an outsider; rather it can be taken as a historical document of the partition presented in the form of a novel. In his autobiography, *Truth, Love & a Little Malice: An Autobiography*, Khushwant Singh recounts that while he was practising law in Lahore, he became part of a literary circle, and that he used his visits to Sikh villages from where his clients came as backgrounds for his stories (S102). He also recalls how, on the eve of the Partition, he had narrowly missed being murdered on his way to Lahore from Abbotabad via Taxila, and how the day after he reached Lahore, he had learnt from the papers that the train by which he had travelled had been held up at the signal near Taxila station and all the Sikh passengers in it were dragged out and murdered (108). This is not an easy task to recount the tales of horrors which tormented him so much. But Singh has shown enough sincerity to portray the painful tales in such a way that it still makes the heart of any reader heavy. Like an historian, Singh mixes his own painful experiences of partition to produce *Train to Pakistan.*

Rushdie's *Midnight's Children*: A Portrayal of Pre- & Post-Partition Subcontinent

Salman Rushdie's Booker Prize winning novel *Midnight's Children* was the first major Indian fiction to get international acclaim. It paved the way for the future generation novelist to take their literary works to the international level. *Midnight's Children* exploits a range of literary and cultural resources from allegory, satire, and surrealism to Hindi cinema, Hindu mythology, science fiction, detective novels, American 'westerns,' political slogans, and advertising jingles (Gopal 91). The importance of the novel as a partition text is not because of its narration of the historical events but because of its highlighting the situation of post-partition. As William Walsh has rightly pointed out, this novel is unprecedented in scope and manner in the history of the Indian novel in English as it deals with the theme of Partition in a very unique manner (122). In fact, of all the Indian English fiction that deals with the partition theme, *Midnight's Children* is the only novel to cover both the 1947 partition that divided India into two separate nations, and the later division in 1971, when East and West Pakistan turned into Pakistan and Bangladesh.

The narrative of the novel begins long before the birth of the protagonist Saleem Sinai. It gradually moves towards the history of modern India depicting the return of Saleem's grandfather Aadam Aziz after his return from Germany to Kashmir in the early twentieth century and the consequent happenings thereafter. Then the narration moves on to the tragic flight of Ahmed Sinai who is Saleem's businessman father in the independent 'secular' India and later in Pakistan. In the concluding part of the novel, the reader comes across the incident of the birth of Ahmed Sinai's son, Aadam, who represents the promise of a more realistic generation than the earlier ones. Interestingly, through these three generations the narrator has succeeded to present the entire history of the Indian subcontinent opening with the 1919-Jallianwalabagh massacre and closing with the internal Emergency of 1975. There are two chapters in Book I of this novel dealing with the incidents of the Partition. One chapter entitled 'Methwold's Estate' is the prelude to the end of Book I, and 'Tick, Tock,' is the last chapter of the first book. Methwold is an unwillingly quitting colonial selling his property in Bombay to a select group of the city's Indian elite before finally leaving India forever. Both Methwold and the selling of his property are significant. He sells his estate having four identical European-style houses named after the royal palaces of Europe on two conditions. One of these conditions, showing his unwillingness to let go his erstwhile holdings, was that the houses should be purchased with all the articles in the houses. The new owners won't be allowed to remove any of these articles. Secondly, the shifting of ownership won't take place until midnight of 15 August. This transfer of ownership of Methwold's estate thus stands both as a metaphor and a parody of the political transfer of power that took place in India during that time. Apart from this, Methwold's significance lies in the fact that he is the biological father of Saleem. Significantly, this incident is a bitter irony to the birth of the nation itself. As Saleem, the illegitimate child of Methwold, turns out to be an Anglo-Indian, it also shows that the independent India, being a product of British rule, will also bear the identity of its colonizer, willingly or unwillingly. Rushdie seems to be arguing that the new state that came into being on 15 August 1947 was Indian in its colour, composition and make-up, but its pedigree was unmistakably British (Roy 93).

It seems Rushdie has questioned the very idea of India. Although India became independent as a result of the collective effort of the people of India, their life-style as a whole did not move in the same direction. Rushdie depicted the fate of Indian Muslims through the fortunes of the Sinai family in the novel showing how they and their relatives moved from one place to another for stability and fortune. Rushdie's own family had suffered similarly in 1947. The novel shows the breaking down and plight of the Muslim community in the subcontinent. For them, neither Independence nor the Partition delivered the desired results. Indeed, the course of events set out in *Midnight's Children* clearly shows that between the so-called secularism of India and the suffocating civic freedoms in Pakistan in the name of Islam, the Muslims of the subcontinent had very little option left. While portraying the second partition, Rushdie gives a vivid picture of the genocide that predated the Bangladesh War of Independence. In fact, the depiction of this second partition of the subcontinent in *Midnight's Children* raises a number of vital questions regarding some of the fundamental issues that were at stake in 1947, and which were in no way resolved by dividing the subcontinent on the basis of religion.

The third part deals with this second division of the subcontinent into Pakistan and Bangladesh. As Book II of the novel sums up the Indo-Pak War of 1965, Book III begins with the 1971 war of East and West Pakistan. There are only three chapters on the Bangladesh War. The first and third chapters state the political development in Pakistan between December 1970 when Mujib-ur-Rahman's Awami League swept the country's polls, and December 1971 when Bangladesh came into being. The events of the five intervening years between 1965 and 1970—both in Pakistan and in Saleem's life—are depicted briefly at the beginning of this section. For Rushdie, the war itself is full of confusion since the parties involved in the war—Pakistan's west wing, east wing and India—are confused about their aims and objectives. The chapters covering Bangladesh in the novel question the very idea of a pan-Indian/pan-Islamic identity. Its War of Independence was full of shocks; Rushdie conveys the dramatic way in which it is extended right from beginning to the end. He depicts how, in March 1971, west Pakistani forces with the help of *Razakars* (crack troops) wreak havoc on innocent civilians in Dacca. There was a dramatic change when in December 1971 the Mukti Bahini volunteers began to terrorize west wing officials and soldiers (the *Khan shena*) alike in east Pakistan. Incidents sped up even more in the novel so that it was all over in three short weeks. At the end, there remained a shattered Pakistan. The chapters that deal with the Bangladesh war give the most piteous show how people are butchered by their own brothers. The brutality of the Bangladesh war is basically a recognition of the extent of the error of the partition and manifests the bitter irony of the intended purpose of partition.

Amitav Ghosh's *The Shadow Lines*: An Urge for Borderless Nation

That Partition has a long-lasting impact on the life and activities of the people of India and Pakistan can be seen in Amitav Ghosh's novel *The Shadow Lines.* In this novel, Amitav Ghosh is more concerned about the aftermath of partition. For Ghosh the partition event has served as a source to explore the concepts like 'freedom' and 'nationalism' that were associated with the idea of partition and to question the very idea of border by introducing the concept of borderless boundary (Roy 113).

The novel shows concern about the partition that influences the nation-building process. Interestingly, the protagonist of Ghosh's novel belongs to the majority community which plays an important role in building up the policies of the nation. On the other hand, the horizon of the novel is much beyond the territory of the nation. Ghosh's novel crosses the limit of time and space far more extensively. Through this movement in this diverse space and time, Ghosh has tried to establish two important ideas of his own—first of all is his idea of a borderless universe and second is his desire for recovering lost histories in the myriad of time. Although it appears the novel has very little to do with the partition but a deep understanding of the novel reveals the fact that the core of the novel lies in the partition of 1947. The death of Tridib actually results from the event of partition that took place far back in 1947 indicating thereby that the aftermath of partition is still visible, even after such a time-gap. The death of Tridib raises doubts to the issue of the unique political reality that exists in the post-1947 Indian subcontinent. The division and the creation of the two newly created states was demarcated on the basis of communal identity cannot solve the existing problem; rather it created a history worsening the communal hatred. Before partition, both the communities lived together as brothers but after the creation of separate nations the same people became each other's enemy. There lies Ghosh's idea of borderless universe. Borders divide not only the land into two parts but also the hearts of people.

The novelist's idea of a borderless universe because borders are insignificant has been established in the novel by three passages. The three protagonists have articulated their opinions in favour of borderless boundary. The first is located in a context wherein it is told that before flying to Bangladesh, Tha'mma felt disturbed to realize that her place of birth (Dhaka, in Bangladesh) is messily at odds with her nationality (Indian). While conversing with her son, she comes to know that the 'border' is not on the frontier, but right inside the airport. This she cannot realise properly. It is difficult for her to believe that no such external marks exist demarcating the border between the two countries. Surprised, she asks her son how people understand that both sides are not the same. For her, everything is as before when she used to catch a train in Dhaka and get off in Calcutta the next day with nobody in between to stop her. Thamma's senile old Jethamoshai provides the second reflection on borders. He was the chief reason behind her Dhaka visit. He provides, surprisingly though, a different standpoint on the Partition. When people insist that he must leave Dhaka with his family to Calcutta, he simply refuses to leave. He asserts that once a person starts moving he can never stop. This harsh reality he could understand quite appropriately. For him, there is no difference between India and Pakistan. Even he went on believing that next day someone else might draw another boundary anywhere and then they would have to fly from there also. Fifteen years after, similar sentiment is echoed by Robi. He was a boy at that time. Fifteen years later, while he relates his version of Tridib's death to the protagonist in London, he is an Indian Administrative Service officer, with first-hand knowledge of many riots and communal disturbances in the subcontinent. He feels the root of all problems seemed to lie with the concept of 'freedom' for everywhere the communities are fighting with each other in the name of freedom. The concept of freedom is a mirage and therefore there will be no difference if someone draws thousands of lines across the globe. What is important to note here is that the above three viewpoints about borders are provided by three characters belonging to three generations. Jethamoshai had lived in a world where borders were not of vital importance; rather one's sense of belonging to the place where one was born and brought up. His words sound prophetic, for within a decade, in 1971, East Pakistan became Bangladesh. Grandma, the other character to ponder on borders, grew up in the tumultuous decades of the twentieth century when the struggle against the British rule in India was at its peak. Struggle was the most formative of her experiences, something that defined her worldview, and Ghosh's narrative makes it clear that though she had not literally participated in the nationalist movement, the spirit of the times had entered her soul and contributed to the creation of her own perception of self. Different, again, is the third speaker on borders, Robi, who as an individual belonging to a post-Partition generation, and having an intimate knowledge of the communally coloured disturbances that destroys the national fabric of India, knows very well how freedom seemed to lie at the very root of all the subcontinent's problems.

The partition theme being a recurring issue in Indian English fiction has always been a matter of attention. But it is quite interesting to see that the handling of partition theme in Indian English fiction has changed from time to time. In the novel of Khushwant Singh, we have seen that the incidents of partition have been mingled with strong nationalist ideology and political events. This must have happened because the author lived during this period and therefore himself was the victim of this. So his description of the partition and its impact is of more practical experiences than philosophical understanding. On the other hand, novelists like Salman Rushdie and Amitav Ghosh have lived far away from the horrible experiences of partition. Therefore, their depiction of partition is much more idealistic. The description of partition may vary from author to author, but the partition as a theme has made possible building up of many such novels which have made Indian English fiction of post-independence rich. These novels are marked by their authenticity, poignant depiction and idealistic views taken from the incidents of partition that have changed the demography and faith of the people of the Indian subcontinent.

Works Cited

Gopal, Priyamvada. *The Indian English Novel: Nation, History, and Narration*. New Delhi: Oxford University Press, 2009.

Hasan, Mushirul. *The Myth of Muslim Unity: Colonial and Nationalist Narratives, in Legacy of a Divided Nation: India's Muslims since Independence*. New Delhi: Oxford University Press, 2001.

Mukherjee, Meenakshi. *The Perishable Empire: Essays on Indian Writing in English*. New Delhi: Oxford India Paperbacks, 2002.

Roy, Rituparna. *South Asian Partition Fiction in English from Khushwant Singh to Amitav Ghosh*. Amsterdam: Amsterdam University Press, 2010.

Singh, Khushwant. *Truth, Love & a Little Malice: An Autobiography*. New Delhi: Penguin, 2002.

Wolpert, Stanley. *Shameful Flight: The Last Years of the British Empire in India*. Oxford: Oxford University Press, 2006.

Walsh, William. *Indian Writing in English*. London: Longman, 1990.

Presentation of Loss and Trauma in Bapsi Sidhwa's *Ice-Candy Man*

PRATAP DEB

Partition, a colonial after mark, was the most fateful event in the history of Indian independence and probably this greatest tragedy of the century came as a crushing blow to the people and more specifically to the minorities of the two provinces of Bengal and Punjab. Freedom along with partition led to a dual picture in the country—somewhere, there was jubilation of Indian independence; while, there was darkness in some other places because of the partition. For millions of people living on both the sides of the border their own motherland became alien for them. People had to leave not only their land and possessions, but also friends, families, and happy memories behind them and had to move towards an unknown destiny and destination.

While discussing about partition the most important thing that comes to our mind is its effect. The afterlife of partition was never the same. It had undergone a sea change. The predominant issues that mark the lives of innumerable peasants are the trauma of loss. Though the term has many different connotations, but our main focus is on the psychology. The individual as well as the collective psychology was disturbed by the suddenness of event.

Bapsi Sidhwa's *Ice-Candy Man* is the story of an eight-year-old lame girl Lenny Sethi which shows how the world around her changes amidst partition. Lenny experiences change in the atmosphere. The usual harmony of the people of different religions soon started being replaced by violence, suspicion and disbelief. All the characters in the novel suffer loss somehow which ultimately creates trauma in their mind.

Commoners in the Indian subcontinent are convinced by then that it was to achieve political mileage the historical event of partition and related genocide took place on eastern and western part of India. The threatened people had to leave their homeland and move to an alien land without knowing what would happen to them. The pain and loss suffered by them can be felt even today.

The aim of this paper is thus not only to study the partition politics, but also to probe into the psychology of the horror reality reflected in the novels, which must attain vitality and dignity. For ordinary people, whose lives were devastated, partition was too high a price. Men and women, victimized during partition, still felt torn. They said: "Now there is no country. Earlier we had a home, a country because we belonged there. Now we belong nowhere . . . the real country is the one we have left behind. That was our real home, the home we loved. Relationships were stronger, families looked after each other. All that has also gone finished." (Menon and Bhasin, 220) Thus, we can see that the very concept of loss and trauma finds an able expression in the works of partition.

Sometimes memory becomes a perennial source of pain and suffering. In her famous book *The Other Side of Silence* Urvashi Butalia reports what Krishna Sobti says about partition: "it is difficult to forget but dangerous to remember" (357). This seems to be true in case of Lenny, who was a mere child when the partition took place. But it was her memory that didn't spare her and haunted her throughout her life.

The concept of 'loss' is closely intertwined with the theme of partition. Partition, which was a man-made tragedy, an event which could have been easily avoided, took its toll on human life displacing innumerable families. Thus, the very concept of loss finds an able expression in the works of partition.

Bapsi Sidhwa's (a leading Pakistani woman-novelist) *Ice-Candy-Man*, which was later made into a film by Deepa Mehta as '1947: Earth,' echoes the same note of desperation, anger and pain. The title *Ice-Candy-Man*, was changed for the American edition by the writer herself because the publishers thought that Americans would misunderstand 'ice-candy' and confuse it with drugs. The new title for the American edition is more explicit and clearly indicates that it is a novel of partition. However, the original title had significant symbolic connotations. First of all, we must remember the centrality of the ice-candy-man's role to the love theme and the political theme of this novel.

The story of *Ice-Candy-Man* presents the picture of the world of a little girl Lenny, and how it changes after the partition. The story records the growth of the child and her memories of partition. Set in Lahore, *Ice-Candy-Man* moves around the life of Lenny Sethi, the daughter of prominent Parsi family who spends her days wandering the streets with her Ayah, her beloved nanny. Her Ayah was very beautiful. *Ice-Candy-Man* is a novel of partition turmoil which includes characters from all communities—Hindus, Muslims, Christians, Sikhs and Parsis. Therefore, a multiple perspective of partition emerges, as it is viewed by all affected people of different religions. However, what really distinguishes Bapsi Sidhwa's *Ice-Candy-Man* is the Parsi sensitivity through which the events are depicted. It is the only novel written by a Parsi on the theme of partition. This makes it unique. The change of attitude of the Parsi community, the impact of violence on the girl-child narrator, the use of allegory and symbolism to depict the horrors of partition, the role of rumour, the dangers of communal frenzy and the rise of fanaticism are the aspects of the partition which get reflected in *Ice-Candy-Man*.

Ice-Candy-Man provides a glimpse into the events and turmoil on the Indian subcontinent during partition. Historic truth forms the backdrop of the novel and the focus is on the individuals and their fate with a special limelight on the character of the ice-candy-man, the deteriorating human relationships and communal discord. Partition, a heart-rending event which is always believed to be affecting millions of lives in many different ways, is shown here as a series of images and events depicting human loss and agony. In rural areas, the Muslim village like Pir Pindo is attacked by the Sikhs. Men, women and children are massacred. Despite this, Bapsi Sidhwa, the sensitive novelist, shows how the humanitarian activities are pursued by individuals like Rodabai, known as Godmother, Lenny's mother and Jagjeet who with a group of Sikhs visit the Muslim village of Pir Pindo under the cover of darkness to warn them of an impending Akali attack. The novelist is also very pragmatic and worldly wise. She shows although individual acts of kindness and bravery can help some victims and lessen their misery but it cannot resist the tide of organized violence.

Lenny, lame in one leg due to an early attack of polio, is reared up by her Ayah. The Ayah is very beautiful and young with a brown complexion. She has "Hindu, Muslim, Sikh, Parsee unified around her" (97). But as the topic of the partition of the country on the communal and religious ground comes up into their conversation, the friendly atmosphere takes a sudden sinister turn. The news of the offending partition disturbs not only the major communities but also the minorities like the Parsis. The usual harmony in Lenny's house too disappears. The Muslim Imam Din, Yousuf, and the ice-candy-man become hostile towards the Hindu Hari and Moti. The Pathan whispers to Ayah about the ominous occurrences in the narrow, crowded alleys of the city.

A sense of distrust grows among them when the talks of a possible partition and the creation of a new nation are on. The suitors are left quarrelling like never before and the harmony between them disintegrates. The most vociferous of all, the ice-candy-man gradually becomes morally bankrupt in the midst of the national crisis.

In the middle of violence, one day during her visit to Imam Din's village, Lenny comes to know about the possible mutual understanding between the Muslims and the Sikhs. The elders in these communities of the nearby villages sit together with a view to bring in peace and harmony in the rural area. The Sikh Granthi says: "Our villages come from the same racial stock. Muslim and Sikh, we are basically Jats. We are brothers. How can we fight each other!" (56)

These reassuring and soothing promises, however, prove futile and unfortunately the same people resort to inhuman atrocities, killing thousands of men and women of both the sides. When the Muslims of Lahore receive the trainload of the Muslim corpses, they turn frantic. Even the ice-candy-man who is till then a good friend of the Hindu Ayah reports angrily the following news: "A train from Gurdaspur has just come in, . . . Everyone in it is dead. Butchered. They are all Muslim. There are no young women among the dead! Only two gunny-bags full of women's breasts." (149)

The Muslims of Lahore attack the Sikhs and the Hindus and then follow the scenes of inhuman atrocities, abduction, rapes, massacres and the resultant migration of the minority of India. Several Hindus and Sikhs are forcibly converted to Islam and some become Christians only to save their lives and property. Hari, the gardener in Lenny's house, becomes Himat Ali and the Hindu Ayah is forcefully kept by the ice-candy-man and so on. It is because of the Ayah that people belonging to all religions came together for some time but due to the partition they get disintegrated. Now, the amount of 'loss' can be measured from the above two instances. First, is the loss of identity of Hari. Name is the primary source of identity for a person he gets from his or her parents. It makes him known to all. Equally important is religion in one's life. But after a life long-lived, if a person is forced to change his or her name and religion s/he is destroyed from within, it becomes equivalent to his/her death. This can be felt and measured only by that person who suffers it. Second is the forceful account brought upon Ayah, a Hindu and moreover a woman. She was a victim in two ways. This seems to be true when the ice-candy-man forcefully keeps the beautiful Hindu Ayah with him as if he has conquered over the Hindus.

Finally, the Ayah opts for India and the Parsee family sticks to the land where they are. A feeling of insecurity makes them rethink about their choice. In fact, they are not sure about their being secure with any religion involved in atrocities. They say: "If we're stuck with the Hindus they'll swipe our business from under our noses and sell our grandfathers in the bargain; if we're stuck with the Muslims they'll convert us by the sword! And God help us if we're stuck with the Sikhs!" (37)

The communal possessions become larger to Lenny's eyes when she reaches the Warris road. At the beginning they do not sound very threatening: the demonstrators are a few tattered youths—mostly street urchins—who disperse to pick the fruit from the trees on the road; their banners are nothing but rags. Lenny and Adi themselves—as though in a game—join the different groups shouting opposite slogans 'Jai Hind! Jai Hind!' or 'Pakistan Zindabad!" (127) as the case may be. This account seems to suggest that the ensuing disaster, lurking in apparently harmless episodes, swoops down almost unawares, as though people were caught in an epidemic mass frenzy, that at a certain point, gets out of hand and becomes greater than its actors themselves. The slogans become louder, more acrimonious and menacing, till the threshold of humanity is crossed and fury is unleashed.

Ayah's body itself becomes a bloody battlefield. Desired by all and ravished by those who courted and loved her, Ayah stands for all those women who suffered the agonies of pre- and post-partition, on whose bodies' disputes were held. Urvashi Butalia throws light on the reason why women and their sexuality were so central in the contentions preceding and following partition. Thus violence against women, carried out brutally and systematically during partition, was not just incidental to it, but generated by particular social structures and cultural values.

It is when the fires subside and slogans seem to have lost their urgency, Ayah is abducted. While the fever of partition is running high, Ayah, who was once in total control of the emotions and actions of her admirers, loses her power. The outburst of violence, the feeling of revenge and suspicion, the departures or conversion of Hindu and Sikh friends make a fearful being of her. She considers leaving Lahore to reach her relatives in Amritsar and when Masseur, whose love for Ayah has not been touched by any resentment or folly built up by partition, is killed, she is lost. Her radiant beauty is dimmed; as Lenny observes, "The glossy chocolate bloom in her skin is losing its sheen." (177)

Lenny's closeness to Ayah becomes almost self-identification with her nanny; the young woman's pain is for the child, a physical sensation, which she cannot fully understand: "And Masseur's death has left in her the great empty ache I know sometimes when the muscles of my stomach retract around hungry spaces within me . . . but I know there is an added dimension to her loss I cannot comprehend. . . . we walk hand in hand two hungry wombs." (177) The young woman in front of her is deprived of herself, and her very name is also a changed one. She looks awkward in all her new make-up and fine clothes, but there is no glowing from inside her.

As she is separated from Lenny's world, the end of Ayah's story remains untold, but through Hamida's story Bapsi Sidhwa represents the fate of most women who suffered rape and abduction and, in the aftermath, found themselves deprived of their identity and of a place in society. Hamida has lost her status of wife and mother; she is now classified as one of the fallen creatures gathered in the camp for recovered women set up by the Government in the evacuated house next to the Sethis. At night she wakes up and listens to the "cries verging on the inhuman" (212), as if it denotes the brutality of their dehumanization. Sidhwa has used animal imagery to express their misery: Lenny compares Hamida with a "starved and grounded bird" (193), a symbol of utter helplessness and the refugee families living in Warris Road are presented like "night animals in the twilight interiors of their lairs, still afraid of being evicted." (190)

Lenny cannot understand Hamida's tears, her constant agonies, but she can clearly feel that her lap is 'rigid' (237); she cannot believe that fate is the cause of the women's wails. In Sidhwa's *Ice-Candy-Man*, partition is shown in a series of images and events depicting human loss and agony. The dislocation of settled life is revealed by Lenny's understanding of the change in Lahore. In utter desperation, Lenny observes that Lahore is no more cosmopolitan. The Sikhs and Hindus have fled. "Lahore is suddenly emptied of yet another hoary dimension; there are no Brahmins with caste-marks or Hindus in dhotis with bodhis. Only hordes of Muslim refugees." (175)

The child narrator senses the difference and pain caused by the huge exchange of populations. The dislocation and uprootedness of partition is experienced by Lenny and her brother Adi as they drift through Queen's Garden searching in vain for familiar faces and acquaintances.

The dislocation of life during Partition caused emotional upheavals. This is best exemplified by the attitude of Lenny when she learns that Masseur, one of Ayah's admirers, has proposed to marry her. Even in the child, there is a feeling of insecurity as she clings to Ayah's hands and cajoles her not to marry the masseur as it would cause separation.

Bapsi Sidhwa subtly delineates the psychological impact of the horrors of partition. The communal frenzy has a distorting effect on people and leads to a feeling of suspicion and distrust—all these are susceptible to rumours. Revenge becomes the major motive for the ice-candy-man and his group of friends. The role of rumour and the consequent pattern of violence shown by Bapsi Sidhwa are very contemporary. Similar patterns are depicted by Amitav Ghosh in his novel *The Shadow Lines*. Using the narrative technique of revealing events by reading old newspaper reports, Amitav Ghosh shows how communal violence is spread in Calcutta and cities of erstwhile East Pakistan since 1964. The poisoning of water, the trains of dead bodies, all incredible rumours, further inflated the communal frenzy.

Ice-Candy Man closes with Ayah's departure for Amritsar, followed by a changed ice-candy-man. Being both gone past extreme boundaries, Ayah, the innocent victim whose identity is by now brutally stripped from her, and the ice-candy-man, the religious fanatic, who has lost the very essence of humanity, separately cross over the newly created border. This seems to be the long cut imagined by Ayah which, according to her, are two throbbing symbols of the loss and trauma ingrained in the fabric of the two nations born from partition. Though the critics often raise the question about the child narrator's perception, yet it stands as a specimen of a neutral Parsi view of partition.

The country divided on communal lines on the eve of Independence brought in its wake the twin traumas—the physical one of being dislocated and forced to migrate and the psychological one of living in 'alien' conditions—which millions of people experienced living on both sides of the border. *Ice-Candy Man,* thus, gives us a searing account of a nation in communal flames. This is probably the first novel in which we get a child's eye view of the horrors of partition experience. Moreover, being a Parsi, it was possible for Sidhwa to observe neutrally the Hindu-Muslim involvement in the pre-partition riots and thereafter. What the author tries to communicate is that in the name of religion the victims are always the common men who are no way responsible for the riots.

Works Cited

Butalia, Urvashi, *The Other Side of Silence*, New Delhi: Penguin, 1998.

Menon, Ritu and Bhasin Kamla. *Borders and Boundaries: Women in India's Partition*. New Delhi: Women Unlimited, 1998.

Sidhwa, Bapsi. *Ice-Candy Man*, New Delhi: Penguin India, 1989.

Re-inventing Myth: A Study of Chitra Banerjee Divakaruni's *The Palace of Illusions*

BANANI CHAKRABORTY

Modern writers are paying homage to the ancient myths and legends of India and reproducing the mythical stories in a new way. Like many such novelists, Chitra Banerjee Divakaruni has tried her hands at re-inventing the mythical epic Mahabharata in her novel The Palace of Illusions. The timeless epic Mahabharata has been told and retold in different languages through a variety of mediums. In this respect, Divakaruni's attempt is not new, but what is unique is that she tells the story in first person narrative through the voice of Panchaali giving her the status of a narrator-heroine or Sutradhari. The great war of the Mahabharata *has been glorified by Veda Vyasa, depicting the war as a battle between the good and the evil where the victory would undoubtedly be of the good. However, Divakaruni reflects the horror and unavoidable destruction caused by war.* The Palace of Illusions *is not merely a retelling of the* Mahabharata, *it is rather a re-invention in the sense that the writer encapsulates the occurrences of the epic in the novelistic genre and inspires the modern readers to find parallels with the modern situation.*

A trend has developed among the Post-Independence Indian English litterateurs to utilise the Indian epics as their source for ancient myths to construct their own fictional world. Living in this high-tech world, they find the mythical stories fascinating, magical and yet relevant to the present situation. India has a rich treasure of mythological stories having admirers across the countries. Mythological stories of the great epics like *the Ramayana* and the *Mahabharata* are not merely tales of Gods, demons, demigods, miracles and mysteries; these also provide us knowledge about the social structure and cultural beliefs of the ancient time and people. Retelling of the Indian mythological stories re-establishes their significance in the modern Indian social context. This article aims at analyzing the mythological novel *The Palace of Illusions* from perspectives like the strategies involved in narrating the novel and its applicability to the modern context in relation to the war-effected situation. This objective will be pursued mainly through the theoretical perspective of myth criticism.

Ashok K. Banker is a prominent literary figure in retelling the myths of the *Mahabharata* and the *Ramayana*, the stories of Krishna and so on. Amish Tripathy, a young Indian writer is so much inspired by the stories of ancient India that he has penned down the myth of Shiva totally from a new outlook, so much so that his debut novel *The Immortals of Meluha* (2010) followed by *The Secret of the Nagas* (2011) have become bestsellers luring the readers of every age-group. However, it is Chitra Banerjee Divakaruni's re-invention of the *Mahabharata* in her novel *The Palace of Illusions* published in 2008 that has enthralled the East-West readers and made them re-think of the events and incidents and issues of the great epic.

Chitra Banerjee Divakaruni is an Indo-American writer well-known for her collection of short stories, poems and fiction. Divakaruni now teaches creative writing at the University of Houston. Despite living in America for a long time, she has not lost her connection with and admiration for Indian tradition and culture; rather she attempts to give this ancient Indian culture a global face. In *The Palace of Illusions,* Divakaruni does not tend to invent a totally new world out of Veda Vyasa's *Mahabharata.* The novel honestly pursues the story-line of the epic without introducing any new character. But, she re-invents those aspects of the mythical epic which otherwise seemed to remain unnoticed so long by the readers. She attempts to focus on those aspects which didn't get much attention in the original narrative. From a different standpoint, she narrates the story and through her simple language and style, Divakaruni appeals to the imaginative as well as the rational mindset of the modern readers. Thus, the mythological story is given a fresh look so as to use the same as a metaphor to interpret the present-day situations.

The *Mahabharata* has been translated from Sanskrit to many different languages. In this respect, Divakaruni's attempt is not new but her uniqueness lies in narrating the story in first person. Here Draupadi whom she calls Panchaali is the narrator. To make her the narrator of all the events, Divakaruni had to empower Panchaali with some special vision and perception. The narrator of the original epic, Vyasa, has also a role in the narrative structure guiding Panchaali build up her narrative through his prophecies. The story begins with Panchaali's birth from fire; it maturates reflecting on the life of Panchaali and ends with her final departure. Telling the story of birth through one's own voice requires a witty craftsmanship and Divakaruni chooses a grandmother as narrator to tell Panchaali the incidents of her childhood days: "Through the long, lonely years of my childhood, when my father's palace seemed to tighten its grip around me until I couldn't breathe, I would go to my nurse and ask for a story. . . . This winter afternoon, sitting cross-legged in the meagre sunlight that managed to find its way through my slit of a window, she said." (1) Thus both Panchaali and the readers are informed about the story of her birth.

As Divakaruni gives a mythological account in her novel, she employs certain facets which are largely applicable to the narrative structure of a myth. According to Frazer, myth should be read literally and be treated as an explanation of certain phenomena (Segal, 35). Ernst Cassirer points out that myth is one way of using language for expressive purposes with the help of some symbolic devices. He argues that mythical thoughts is a mode of symbolically structuring the world and that myth should be treated as relating to the process of mind as projected on to the world. This idea of projection makes one think logically of the psychoanalytic theories of myth (Segal, 36). The basic tenet of the psychoanalytic theories of Freud and Jung is the assumption that the symbols of myth as well as the themes of its plot are constructed in the unconscious. According to Jung, the symbolic structure of the unconscious is a reality which cannot be totally reduced to any other level of experience. However, the Freudian theorists treat myth as the expression of mental forces. This treatment possesses the idea that myths are like day-dreams. It involves the process of dream-work that symbolically reconstructs messages emitted from the unconscious. The message here is not explicit but disguised and the body of message is condensed.

In *The Palace of Illusions*, Divakaruni gives a series of messages through her protagonist's dreams. With the help of her unusual dreams, Panchaali is conscious of many of the events which otherwise would have been unknown to herself as well as to the readers. One of the most significant dreams that can be mentioned in this respect is her dream of Karna and Kunti. In her dream, Panchaali could not immediately recognize the shawl-wrapped lady as Kunti but she recognized Karna even before she could see his face. This dream arouses suspicion in Panchaali's mind as to why Kunti would go to meet her sons' enemy by the river side so secretly. Soon Panchaali discovers the truth about Karna and Kunti's real relationship. The device of dream has been skilfully employed as an agent in the narrative structure of the novel by Divakaruni to communicate what would remain otherwise inexpressible. In Chapter 34 of the novel Panchaali recalls her dream hearing Karna's conversation with Bheeshma: "Suddenly, everything that had puzzled me began to make sense" (273).

Other than this dream, Panchaali's dream of the 'palace of lac' in Chapter 15 of the novel and her last but most painful dream of Aswatthama killing her most beloved children and brothers also render important messages in a condensed manner.

The dreams apparently appear to be a representation of the unconscious; however, these dreams have been given a good space in the narrative structure and are weighed with significant meanings. According to the psychoanalytic theory of myth, these dreams are utilised as mythical symbols. These symbols express a universal concern for themes such as the process of physical and psychological incorporation and expulsion, the fear of abandonment and destruction, rivalry between parent and child and between parent and siblings etc. Rendering such voluminous connotations, the dream narratives fashion Divakaruni's rewriting of the epic in the form of a novel in a unique way.

Though an adaptation of the *Mahabharata*, Chitra Banerjee Divakaruni's narrative technique is quite different from the original epic written in verse-form. She has woven myth in the structure of the novel. This strategy can precisely be said as the technique known as story within a story. Within the structure of one story, another story is told, thereby giving the narrative a multi-layered structure. Whereas the same stories in Veda Vyasa's *Mahabharata* can be studied as a story within a story intended to depict philosophical knowledge or knowledge about Dharma, Divakaruni's can be studied as a structural device that does not impose any didactic lesson but let it open to the readers to interpret and appreciate the same and relate them to the main story.

A story within a story is basically a literary device in which more than one narrative is interwoven simultaneously. One action is presented during the course of another action. This literary device can be used in different literary forms like novels, short stories, plays, poems, philosophical essays and so on. A writer can use this device as a tool of entertainment or to act as an example to the characters outside the inner story. The stories often carry psychological as well as symbolic significance for the characters of the inner story. One such inner story Chitra Banerjee Divakaruni takes from the *Mahabharata* is the tale of Nal and Damyanti. Divakaruni sets the background for the narration of the story with a sort of introduction: "To divert our minds from our misfortunes, they told us stories of people whose sufferings were far worse. . . . My favourite was the story of Nal and Damyanti, perhaps because of its parallels to our life. . . . This is the story, in the bareness of bones." (208)

The story of Nal and Damyanti was told by one of the sages who used to visit the Pandavas during their exile in the forest. The sage's intention to tell the story was to give a lesson to the Pandavas so that they learn to bear their misfortunes valiantly. Whereas Yudhistir's perception of the story was from one symbolic angle, Panchaali's perception was from another angle which is more akin to her deep insight: 'Yudhistir didn't seem to see' (208) the parallel to the story of the Pandavas. Nal, the Nishad king had lost every single bit of his possession and even his kingdom to his brother just as Yudhistir lost his own. Despite losing the last piece of cloth, Nal did not wager his beloved wife. Damyanti also supported her husband in his adversity. But, Nal left the sleeping Damyanti in the forest, thinking it to be the best for her to get rid of the calamities brought upon her because of him. It is because of Damyanti's conviction and determination to search for and get her husband back that they were united after a long span of years. After the narration of this inner story, Divakaruni elevates her story to the level of an impressionistic narrative. The virtuous Yudhistir brought out the symbol of righteousness from the story, saying: "Look, how Nal never swerved from righteousness, no matter what happened. And Damyanti never rebuked him for his losses but gave him all the support a man needs when in trouble" (209). However, Panchaali interprets the story through her psychological perception in a different way: "How did Nal repay her? By abandoning in a forest? How was that righteous?" (209) The answers are not given in the structure of the narrative and the readers are equally free to interpret the story as per their own perceptions.

Thus, the story woven inside the main story bears a symbolic and psychological significance to the characters. Such an impact had the story on Panchaali that she could not keep Damyanti out of her mind. She was amazed to think of the courageousness of Damyanti: "How frightened she must have been—and how brave. Because she didn't go back to her parents right away. Instead, she searched for Nal for years. Once she was stoned to death as a witch—she, a princess who had been famed the world over for her beauty." (209) And from there, the narrative captures the intellection of Yudhistir, the other character, as Panchaali travels from the thought of Yudhistir to that of her own: "I was no ideal wife. . . . She was better than I" (208)

In the construction of the novel, Chitra Banerjee Divakaruni narrates the past lives of some of the characters, like that of Bheeshma and Shikhandi. However, the myth of the past lives of these characters is not directly narrated by the main narrator herself. She is twice disconnected from this narrative to play either the role of a listener or of an eavesdropper. She gets aware of Bheeshma's past life by eavesdropping on the conversation between Karna and Bheeshma. The narrative of one's past life would definitely arouse questions in the mind of any rationalistic modern reader. However, Divakaruni skilfully incorporates these questions in the narrative structure, which are asked by none other than the narrator herself. The power and truth behind every myth is questioned time and again by the inquisitive scholars throughout the world. As readers, we seek answers to the questions that are raised in our minds regarding the myths related to our social, cultural and religious life; so does Panchaali, a mythological character and the narrator of the novel. She questions the truth about Shikhandi's past life repeatedly: "Could he really be Amba in a previous incarnation?" (49)

James Frazer in *The Golden Bough* observes the death-rebirth myth as the representative of the growing envisions and agriculture, whereas Carl Gustav Jung envisions the death-rebirth archetype as symbolic expression taking place not in the world but in the mind. That process, according to him, is the temporary "return of the ego to the unconscious—a kind of temporary death of the ego and its re-emergence or re-birth from the unconscious. This concept of Jung leads to the idea of collective unconscious" (Segal, 4). This theoretical concern can be applied logically to Divakaruni's narrative on the theme of re-birth which she employs on Krishna's comment made in reply to Panchaali's question regarding the truth of Shikhandi's past life: "He believes it to be so. Isn't that what truth is? The force of a person's believing seeps into those around him—into the very earth and air and water." (49) Allan W. Watts in his *Myth and Ritual in Christianity* (1954) observes: "Myth is to be defined as a complex of stories—some no doubt fact and some fantasy—which for various reasons, human beings regard as demonstrations of inner meaning of universe and of human life" (7).

How far the meaning of the universe and of human life is demonstrated is questionable; but these myths and stories interwoven in the main narrative of the novel provide hopes and lessons to many. Bheeshma's past life, as he admits, taught him a lesson for lifetime, whereas Shikhandi's knowledge about his past life gave him a sort of hope or more precisely cause to ignite his thirst for revenge.

Chitra Banerjee Divakaruni, through *The Palace of Illusions* aims at attracting every twenty-first century modern reader across the world. For this purpose, narrating the story in an epic form would have been too ambitious a project. As she shifts from one literary genre to another, so does she shift from the typical narrative technique of the *Mahabharata* in verse form to her own multifarious techniques. The verse narrative of the *Mahabharata* consists of 48,000 lines but Divakaruni's re-invention of the epic is totally in prosaic form and concisely it records the important aspects of the epic. Like Vyasa, she does not divide the novel into Eighteen Parvas; rather she divides the novel into forty three chapters keeping thematic relevance to the original epic. Divakaruni pursues the oral narrative technique, the revelation of the reason behind King Drupad and Drona's enmity is one such example where different assumptions are made by Dhri and Panchaali through argument and counter-argument. As Panchaali starts the story like a professional story teller, Dhri interrupts saying, "No! No! The story must start early. You are looking at the story through the wrong window" (15). However, such interruptions do not stop Panchaali and she proceeds with her story: "You are too partial. . . . I am taking back the story. (15-16)

Thus, the mood of storytelling becomes an integral part of Divakaruni's narrative strategy in *The Palace of Illusions.* Though one narrator, that is, Panchaali has been given the most prominence in the course of the novel, multiple voices come to play their roles, thus conforming to the principle of heteroglossia. The narrative strategy of a literary product is a very important facet for its success. Laxmi Venkatesh in her review of *The Palace of Illusions* writes, "Divakaruni has managed to bind all the characters and the story together through the bold and enticing narrative style."

Divakaruni's re-invention of the myth of the *Mahabharata* focuses intensively on the destructive consequences of war. War is a product of vengeance and the issue of vengeance can be traced in *The Palace of Illusions* from the very beginning. King Drupad performed the great sacrificial yajna to be blessed with a son *who* could avenge him. Thus, the birth of Dhristadyumna along with Draupadi sets off the journey of war. It was prophesized by Vyasa much before the greatest war of the *Mahabharata* that Panchaali would be remembered for causing that greatest war. However, a reading of Divakaruni's reinvention of the Great Epic brings out the fact that the seeds of war were sown even before her birth. King Drupad, who was defeated by Drona, wanted to defeat him in turn. Shikhandi wanted a battle in which he could kill Bheeshma. The Kaurava brothers, at enmity with the Pandavas, wanted just a scope to call for a battle and to drive them away from the kingdom. All these repressed intentions found a way of ventilation when Panchaali cursed the Kauravas in the Sabha and vowed to bathe in their blood. Thus, everybody wanted the war, but very few thought of its after-effect. "War is like avalanche. Once begun, it cannot cease until it has wreaked all the destruction it is capable of" (263).

Whereas Vyasa's *Mahabharata* glorifies the Great War that destroyed the evil and helped to establish a righteous Kingdom, Divakaruni's rewriting of the great story makes a commentary on the devastation caused by war. While reading the painful account of the war, the readers don't feel like having an account of the unknown mythical past, rather they feel its impact, because every reader of the modern generation, who is the product of the war-torn world can identify herself with the situation. The premonition of the situation that would follow the Great War recurs throughout the novel. Thus reference of war becomes a recurrent myth as human beings have witnessed the misery and misfortune after every war since the ancient time. Whereas primitive men fought battles to bring back natural order of life and mythological war signifies the victory of good over evil, the modern wars are fought to assert power and impose supremacy of one nation over the other. For whatever reasons the war may take place, the post-war situation is almost the same.

In the essay *Theories of Myth,* Percy. S. Cohen discusses that the myth-making mind uses any material that it instantly gets. But this activity involves drawing materials from hidden places, and this process of drawing materials has a magic quality about it. If myth is the way of anchoring the present in the past, then it will draw to it the symbols of past which resides in most human minds. War, thus becomes a symbol taken from myth that Chitra Banerjee Divakaruni employs to connect to the present condition of human minds of the twenty first century. The devastating effect of the war of the *Mahabharata* can be identified with the impact of the First World War, Second World War and many other wars like that of the America-Iraq war. The world wars spread death and destruction throughout the world to a great extent. Innumerable people lost their lives, homes, lands and became refugees. The world economy also collapsed as a result of this. The impact of the world war carried forward generation after generation, so much so that children are still born with deformities in Japan as a result of the impact of atom bomb. The Second World War had filled the world with hopelessness, despair and spiritual degeneration. Eliot's *Waste Land* (1922) which is full of mythical references captures such degeneration in a symbolic way. The loss, destruction and violence of war could be felt by different countries several times. The America-Iraq war is a burning example of this. The long-drawn war not only affected those who died fighting the battle, but also left an everlasting mark on those who are living with the memory of loss in the war. If this is taken to be the modern context, then it comes in perfect confrontation with the war-torn situation of the mythical past. Divakaruni records the meaninglessness of war, which becomes appropriate in the context of any war, in the following words: "The land stretched sick and disrobed, great, gaping holes torn into its side by the blasts of astras. The few remaining trees were lifeless skeletons . . . only vultures sat on dead branches, waiting in eerie silence. This was what we had done to our earth" (300).

The account of the *Mahabharata* battle that Divakaruni gives through her spokesperson Panchaali is comprehensive. This account encapsulates the war from its preparatory period to the end. If men and Gods were busy with their own diplomacies to fight the battle, women were no less bothered with challenges: "We women—no less than the men—were going to be faced by challenges we'd never imagined. . . . Who we were as individuals was receding to the background. What mattered more was that our dear ones were going to fight beside each other. From now on we would be united in our anxiety, in being torn between pride and concern, in our prayers for the safety of them all." (247-48)

When the war ended, women were left with no reliable dependence. Whereas some women sacrificed themselves in the funeral pyres of their husbands, some went on to live the burden of life with their painful memories. No veneration but condemnation of war has been emphasized persistently in *The Palace of Illusions.* The violence and pain of war, the physical battle and conflicts within the warriors, the terrible outcome of war are the issues in the novel that appear to be a story of the mythical past. In Chapter Thirteen of the novel, the writer expresses the helpless condition that followed the Great War which has resemblances with the modern predicament of war: "Hastinapur after the war was largely a city of women, widows who had never dreamed that the survival of their families would depend on them . . . t hey were without male protection, they found themselves exploited. . . . Women became unpaid servants. Sometimes they were turned out. . . . There were others that I didn't but I heard of the street corners they frequented at night, selling the only thing left to them. It was a terrible situation" (322-23).

Even a myth gives the reference that no war between good and evil can be fought with perfect righteousness. The question of righteousness which recurs in the novel time and again has many times been seen to succumb to the power of immorality. Thus, the process of killing Abhimanyu was against the rule of war and this was followed by a series of unlawful killings like that of Jayadrath (the illusion of a false sunset created by Krishna betrayed him), Drona (the false news of his son being killed made him let down the weapons), Karna, the most helpless victim (killed when he was without armour), Duryodhan (he was hit with a mace on his thigh). War is thought to be a Kshatriya pride, but the pride becomes an irony in such cases. But justification to such dishonesty in mythological wars too is given. The evil must be destroyed by any means. Even after the evil is destroyed, can the good remain untouched or unaffected by the calamity and suffering of war? This is the question that underlies Divakaruni's handling of the narrative of war.

The myth of war as an agent has been employed by Divakaruni in a distinctive manner to give a sense of futility of it to the modern readers. War turns man into a butcher and insinuates the "drama of hate." The irony of war is that it is not as "civilized," "glory giving" and "great" as it is supposed to be. The war poems of Siegfried Sassoon and Wilfred Owen uncover the hidden disgust behind war. The soldiers and warriors were forced to fight in the name of patriotism and nationhood. The passivity of common soldiers who fought the Mahabharata war has been portrayed in *The Palace of Illusions* as well: "those soldiers had chosen to join my husbands because they supported our cause. Now I realized that for many of them, it was merely a job, an alternative to poverty and starvation. Or maybe they'd been forcibly conscripted by their overlords" (257).

It is not that the Kaurava-army had only been swept away in the battle of bloodshed, but the second generation of the Pandavas too was brutally killed in the battle. But for the unborn child of Abhimanyu, the Pandava clan would have been obliterated. Panchaali is left with the realization that 'she who sows vengeance must reap its bloody fruit' (306). As Devdutt Patnaik points out, "Myth is essentially a cultural construct, a common understanding of the world that binds individuals and communities together" (xvi).

This mythical perception of Panchaali can influence the minds of the modern people to keep them away from war and develop a sense of brotherhood and comradeship to bind the individuals of the societies together. The absurdity of war is a recurrent myth in many literary pieces. Rosencrantz in Act III, sc. iii of Shakespeare's *Hamlet* makes a very significant comment that is applicable to the war in the epic or in the novel and to war taking place between the nations of modern days. He asserts that majesty does not die alone but like a gulf, it draws everything that is close to it. A war can never be fought only between the rulers (Shakespeare, 135). Thus, the Mahabharata war was not only fought between the Pandavas and the Kauravas, not only the fate of the royal descendents was decided by the war, but also thousands of common people were sacrificed. Women became widows, children became fatherless. The land of

Hastinapur and that of its neighbouring territories became waste and barren lands of the dead and the destitute. It is in the *Stree Parva* of the *Mahabharata* that Vyasa comments how the women mourned the deaths of their kinsmen and in *The Palace of Illusions,* the Thirtieth Chapter *Pyre* records the miserable situation of the mourners: "Constant pitiless, ever increasing, the stench assaulted as we made our reluctant way to the battlefield to deal with our dead. I pressed my lips to keep from vomiting. Where earlier soldiers had built their cook fires, now funeral pyres were being lighted—so many that the vista in front of us was covered in a haze of smoke" (310).

Duryodhan's last words to Yudhistir are philosophical in nature that reveals the true state of the post-war situation. No matter who wins, the misery of war would haunt the ruler: "You'll rule a kingdom peopled with widows and orphans and wake each morning to the grief of loss. Who's the real winner, then, who the loser?" (309) Such post-war situation is a bitter truth in any society that has gone or will undergo the experience of war—be it past, present or future.

Percy S. Cohen in the *Theories of Myth* observes that myths perform several functions. They contain layers of meanings that achieve an intuitive experience. Myths are narrated with time anchored structure, because they deal simultaneously with the socially and psychologically significant aspects. They link a sense of deeper level of reality of the past to the present (Segal, 49-50). This is why man makes myths as these contain significance and hence they also share myths. This re-invention of the myth of the *Mahabharata* by Chitra Banerjee Divakaruni can be a sharing of myth and the account of the post-war situation of the Mahabharata battle links the past to the present, as the present world is also a war-torn one.

Devdutt Patnaik claims that "there is no evidence of a perfect world, a perfect man or perfect family anywhere on the earth. Perfection, be it Rama Rajya or Camelot, exists only in mythology. Yet everyone craves for it. This craving inspires art, establishes empires, sparks revolutions and motivates leaders. Such is the power of myth. (Myth = Mithya, xvi)

It seems to be the inspiration gathered from the mythology of the *Mahabharata* that motivated Chitra Banerjee Divakaruni to represent this Great Myth in a new way. So she deals with the problem of an individual regarding her identity in *The Palace of Illusions*, which in the original narrative did not seem to have so much attention. In the middle of the novel, Panchaali seems to be puzzled regarding her identity: "The princess who longed for acceptance, the guilty girl whose heart wouldn't listen, the wife who balanced her fivefold role precariously, the rebellious daughter-in-law, the queen who ruled in the most magical of palaces, the distracted mother, the beloved companion of Krishna, who refused to learn the lessons he offered, the women obsessed with revenge—none of them were true Panchaali. If not, who was I?" (229)

However, it is at the end of the novel that Panchaali finds herself above the gender-biased identity in the patriarchal world. Divakaruni has provided her a new heaven. Draupadi was initially rejected to climb the stairs of heaven as a result of her partiality to love for Arjun. But, Panchaali in *The Palace of Illusions* is above such patriarchal laws. She enjoys the divine blessing of Krishna and is raised beyond the bindings of gender: "I am beyond gender and the imprisoning patterns of ego. And yet, for the first time I'm truly Panchaali" (360).

Many critics have argued that *The Palace of Illusions*, though a retelling of the *Mahabharata,* lacks a detailed study of many events and characters which, if included, would have been wiser on the part of the novelist. In this regard, it can be said that all the aspects of an epic may not be reflected in a novel with great details and so Divakaruni didn't aim at going through the details of the *Mahabharata* and record a personal account of all the characters of the epic. Chitra Banerjee Divakaruni does not only bring the ancient culture into existence, but also gives a new perspective to the mythical epic. Instead of a simple retelling of an ancient text, her work becomes a re-invention in the sense that she endows Draupadi with the characteristic of what can be called a narrator-heroine or *Sutradhari*; she has renewed the epic by encapsulating it in the novelistic genre with the help of lucid language and simple style of narration. Being a modern writer, she also tends to make the readers of her era find parallels of their present condition to that of the mythical past. Thus, to read *The Palace of Illusions* is to re-read the *Mahabharata*.

Works cited

"Archetypal Literary Criticism." Wikipedia, the Free Encyclopaedia.

Bhattacharya, Tania. "Retelling of the Legends," *The Telegraph*| Graphiti. Kolkata, 6.3. 2011. www.telegraphindia.com/110306/jsp

Divakaruni, Chitra Banerjee. *The Palace of Illusions.* New York: Picador India. 2011.

Patnaik, Devdutt. *Myth= Mythya, A Handbook of Hindu Mythology.* New Delhi: Penguin India. 2006.

Sagal, Robert A: *Myth, Critical Concepts in Literary and Cultural Studies*, Vol. 2. Routledge. 2007.

Shakespeare, William. *Hamlet,* Delhi: Oxford University Press, 1999.

"Story within a Story." Wikipedia, the Free Encyclopaedia. Dec. 2007.

Tripathy, Amish. *The Immortals of Meluha.* Chennai: Westland, 2010.

Tripathy, Amish. *The Secret of the Nagas*. Chennai: Westland, 2011.

Venkatesh, Laxmi. *The Palace of Illusions*, A Review. Blah. 10 Mar. 2011. http:/blahmagazine.in/2011/03/9.palace-of-illusions

Watts, Allan W. *Myth and Ritual in Christianity*. New York: Grove Press, 1954.

Wilfred, L. Guerin. *A Handbook of Critical Approaches to Literature.* New York: OUP,.1992.

Mingled Yarn: History and Myth in Amish Tripathi's *The Immortals of Meluha, Part 1* of the Shiva Trilogy

PARTHA SARATHI GUPTA

This paper attempts to investigate into the reasons behind the recurrence of history and mythology in Indian-English fiction, with writers such as Kunal Basu, Chitra Banerjee Divakaruni, Manini Chatterjee and Amish Tripathi exploring the undercurrents of alternate narratives within the grand narratives of mythology and recorded history of ancient, medieval and modern India. In the light of Amit Chaudhuri's reassessment of Indian English fiction in the postcolonial era as an alternative to the conventional English novel, this paper takes up Amish Tripathi's best-seller The Immortals of Meluha, *Part 1, to explore the conscious attempts on the part of contemporary Indian-English novelists to represent the inescapably Indian through alternate modes of discourse in fiction writing, traditionally entrenched in Western notions of realism.*

Writing fiction based on history, myth, and legends seems to be the new fashion in the supermarket of fiction. Since the beginning of the new millennium, readers have been served with doses of history topped with fiction through re-workings of ancient and medieval myths and historical documents, in quick succession, so as to naturally titillate the inquisitive bone of the scholar of literature, throwing open questions on the conditions facilitating such literary productions. The present study is the fallout of readings of such novels in succession beginning with Kunal Basu's *The Miniaturist* and *The Opium Clerk*, Chitra Banerjee Divakaruni's *The Palace of Illusions*, and Amish Tripathi's *The Immortals of Meluha, Part 1.* While the ardent reader of fiction waits eagerly for Tripathi's sequel to Part 1 of the Meluha trilogy about to be released by the end of July 2011, a few illuminating remarks made by an assiduous worker in the field of fiction—Amit Chaudhuri—may help us find a clue to this penchant for myth among contemporary writers of fiction in English in India. In an essay titled "Huge Baggy Monster: Mimetic Theories of the Indian Novel after Rushdie," first published in the *Times Literary Supplement*, 1999, Chaudhuri observes, "Post-Rushdie, the Indian novel in English has been constructed, in both popular and critical terms, as something distinct from—indeed, as alternative to—the conventional English novel" (115). He then goes on to explain:

> A related way of assigning a fundamental Indianness, even non-Westernness, to the postcolonial Indian novel in English is to place its 'magical' subject matter and its expansive, non-realist narrative mode in the lineage of epics such as the *Ramayana* and the *Mahabharata*, and texts like the *Thousand and One Nights*. (116)

This 'magical' subject matter as mentioned by Chaudhuri happens primarily to refer to ancient myths and legends of the Indian subcontinent where myths have always enjoyed a high status. In ancient India, myths have had more discursive power than history. History writing, as we have learnt in Western epistemologies, had been unheard in India. According to Romila Thapar:

> European scholars searched for histories of India but could find none that conformed to the familiar European view of what a history should be, a view influenced in part by the thinking of the European Enlightenment. The only exception according to them was the twelfth century history of Kashmir, the *Rajtarangini*, written by Kalhana. (1)

In fact Kalhana's *Rajtarangini* (A.D. 1149-50) has been the only available work of historical writing in the repertoire of ancient India. Thapar further observes:

> Indian civilization was described as a-historical. Not only were there no histories of India, but the absence of history was also explained by arguing that the concept of time in early India was cyclic. This was inimical to a historical perspective that required each event to be seen as unique, a view endorsed by a linear concept where time moves not in a circle but in a straight line, from a given beginning to a stipulated end. (2)

Myths, thus, in the absence of the discourse of history, have risen to the cause of reconstructing the past, and sometimes could boast of purity of representation. Myths, according to Ashis Nandy, have more explanatory power than history, "because they faithfully contain history, because they are contemporary and unlike history, are amenable to intervention, myths are the essence of a culture, history being at best superfluous and at worst misleading" (59). Contemporary fiction writers in English in the post *postcolonial* world of literature in India have reasonably experimented with the fusion of myth and history, with aplomb. Such myths may be termed misleading and misconstrued by purists, but we must not forget what Ashis Nandy reminds us: that myths are "amenable to intervention" (59), themselves being offshoots of fiction. The back cover of Amish Tripathy's latest novel *The Immortals of Meluha*, Book 1 of the 'Shiva Trilogy,' in a nutshell, draws the reader into the world of history coupled with myth.

> 1900 B.C. In what modern Indians mistakenly call the Indus Valley Civilisation. The inhabitants of that period called it the land of Meluha—a near perfect empire created many centuries earlier by Lord Ram, one of the greatest monarchs that ever lived. This once proud empire and its Suryavanshi rulers face severe perils as its primary river, the revered Saraswati, is slowly drying to extinction. They also face devastating terrorist attacks from the east, the land of the Chandravanshis. To make matters worse, the Chandravan-

> shis appear to have allied with the Nagas, an ostracized and sinister race of deformed humans with astonishing martial skills. The only hope for the Suryavanshis is an ancient legend: 'When evil reaches epic proportions, when all seems lost, when it appears that your enemies have triumphed, a hero will emerge.'

This hero, as Amish narrates, is none other than Shiva, the 'neelkantha,' with a blue throat. In this novel, he must not be confused with the 'nataraj' or the Maheshwar, one of the Trinities of ancient Hindu myth. Here he is just a non-descript Tibetan immigrant from Mount Kailash, near Mansarovar Lake who is summoned by a superior race, the Meluhans of the South, to lead the Suryavanshi vengeance, and destroy evil. Amish in his fiction portrays Shiva as a simple man, drawn to the intoxicating odour of marijuana, wrapped in a 'chillum,' whose karma re-cast him as our Mahadev, the God of Gods in Hindu legend. Events and incidents that have no mythic or historical credibility have been carefully crafted following the age-old Aristotelian principles of 'probability' and 'necessity' to generate a willing suspension of disbelief. Amish achieves his effect by weaving a magical web of received historical data, popular myths and legends from the Puranas, and most importantly, fiction. The reader imaginatively walks into history as the Indus-Valley and the pre-Vedic landscapes come alive, out of history text books in the land of Meluha.

The story of the novel begins in the violent war-ravaged Himalayan region at the foot of Mount Kailash, torn apart by blood-curdling strifes between the mountainous tribes of the region. Shiva is the newly designated chief of the *guna* tribe, fighting for survival in the midst of blood-thirsty war-mongers, especially the Pakratis, who, as we learn "are getting stronger every year, forming new alliances with new tribes." Under these circumstances, they are greeted by an invitation by a superior race, the Meluhans, from down south, and the richest and most powerful empire in the whole world. The invitation is that of an immigration offer for the entire guna tribe. Shiva is at first sceptical of the offer, as the foreign messenger declares:

> You will be given fertile land and resources for farming. Today your tribe, the gunas fight for survival in this rough, arid land. Meluha offers you a lifestyle beyond your wildest dreams. We ask for nothing in return. Just live in peace, pay your taxes and follow the laws of the land. (3)

The foreign messenger is none other than Nandi, who is about to become a disciple of Shiva in the story. Shiva finally agrees to immigrate along with his tribe, but the scepticism remains in his heart as to why the Meluhans chose the Gunas to immigrate and not the violent Pakratis. As they march continuously for four days, the caravan of invited immigrants crosses over to Srinagar, coming across on the way the mighty Jhelum, one of the rivers of the land of the Saptasindhu. After a few routine sanitation rituals in Srinagar, the band is lead towards the city of Devagiri, the Meluhan capital, on the way to which the band comes across several thrilling moments of military adventures that expose the volatility and vulnerability of the body politic of Meluha. The emperor of the land, with whom Shiva is later introduced, is Daksha, whose primary objective is to establish a Suryavanshi way of life across India, which is considered ethical and civilized. But the chief obstacles to the fulfillment of Daksha's objective are the Chandravanshi terrorists, aided by the demonic Nagas, described as "supernatural, blood-thirsty killers!" (272). In a conversation between Shiva and Nandi, on their way to Devagiri, Nandi's description of the Chandravanshis is coloured by a sense of 'othering':

> 'They are cursed people, my Lord,' gasped Nandi. 'They are born with hideous deformities because of the sins of their previous births. Deformities like extra hands or horribly misshapen faces. But they have tremendous strength and skills. The Naga name alone strikes terror in any citizen's heart. They are not even al-

> lowed to live in the Sapta Sindhu. . . . The city of the Nagas exists to the south of the Narmada, beyond the borders of our lands.' (66)

In the course of their conversation the reader is provided with extensive descriptions of the city of Devagiri that strikingly matches with the archaeological and anthropolical evidences in our history books. The Meluhan city sprawling over three giant platforms named Tamra, Rajat and Swarna, rising above the flood plains below, are fictional clues for the readers' identification of these evidences to the urban culture of the Mohenjodaro and Harappan civilizations. Romila Thapar in her essay "A Possible Identification of Meluhha, Dilmun and Makan," observes:

> There could be two possible identifications for Meluhha. One would be to the north or north-west of Sind allowing access to the lapis lazuli trade. . . . Alternately it could be identified with the sea board of western India. If it was the former, then it would be approximately to the west of the Harappa culture, whereas if it was the latter, it would not be to the west but would certainly be at the extremity of the area of distribution of Harappan sites. (280)

The author's fictional construction of the city of Devagiri, the capital of Meluha matches with the former territory identified by Thapar, but the Meluhan empire stretches far south to the coastal city of Karachapa visited by Shiva, the protagonist of Amish's novel on a tour of the Meluhan territory. Shiva, for the first time in his life is mesmerized by the sight of the sea when escorted by Jhooleshwar, the governor of Karachappa, on his very first visit to the coastal city:

> Shiva had never seen the sea and was fascinated by the near infinite expanse of the water. He spent many hours at the port where Jhooleshwar (the Vaishya governor of Karachapa) proudly expounded on the various types of ships and vessels manufactured at the shipyard attached to the Karachapa port. Brahaspati accompanied them to the port to check on the imports due for him from the Mesopotamian merchants. (238)

As is evident from the narrative, here the descriptions of the port city of Karachapa matches with Thapar's identification of the second possible geographical location of *Meluhha* that had been a business hub during the days of the Indus Valley civilization. The name of Meluhha as noted by Thapar has been found in several Mesopotamian records as the possible eastern extremity of Mesopotamian geography. "Economic documents of the Third Dynasty of Ur (2113-2006) refer to the import of copper, ivory, carnelian and onions from both Meluhha and Makan. . . . Meluhha was apparently a coastal area, hence the reference to sailors and maritime people." (Thapar, 278-79).

The simplicity of the Meluhans, the architecture of their buildings, particularly the temples and the Great Public Bath, have all been incorporated by the author to nostalgically carry the ordinary reader of fiction through a journey into the geography of ancient India. The reference to the river Saraswati as the bone of contention between the Chandravanshis and Suryavanshis is also a brilliant collage of history and myth of ancient India. The following extract from an early chapter of the novel introduces us to the cultural indispensability of the river that was unfortunately drying up.

> The capital city of the Meluhans stood on the west bank of the Saraswati, which emerged at the confluence of the Sutlej and Yamuna rivers. Sadly the Saraswati's flow was severely reduced compared to her once mighty size. . . . Unlike many of the tempestuous rivers of the Punjab, the Saraswati was achingly calm. The river seemed to sense that her days were coming to an end. Yet she did fight aggressively to thrust her way through and survive. Instead, she unselfishly gave all to those who came to seek her treasures. (66-67)

The Saraswati comes back as a major fictional centre in Chapter 7 of the novel once again when emperor Daksha explains to Shiva the importance of Saraswati to the Meluhans, who owe their superiority to her, for, from the holy waters of the river, the Somras, a divine medicinal drink was produced. The Somras, as claimed by the Suryavanshi Meluhans, was an elixir produced in a secret location called Mount Mandar by the Meluhans from the waters of the Saraswati that guaranteed their superiority as a race. Daksha tells Shiva:

> The Chandravanshis realized that it was the Somras that guaranteed our superiority. Funnily enough, even they have the knowledge of the Somras. But they have not learnt to produce it like we do and hence haven't reaped all the benefits of it. (118-19)

Daksha also describes the course of river Saraswati from the confluence of the Sutlej and the Yamuna, for the knowledge of Shiva, and how the Chandravanshis changed the course of the river in order to deprive the Suryavanshis of their privilege. "They diverted the course of the Yamuna so that instead of flowing South, it started flowing east to meet their main river, Ganga." (120). The Chandravanshis however provided a different logic behind the drying up of the Saraswati:

> They claimed that the river made such a dramatic change in its course all by itself, due to some minor earthquake. And even worse, they claimed that since the river had changed course of its own accord, we Meluhans would simply have to accept what was essentially God's will! (120)

The Meluhans, as Daksha narrates, even fought a war with the Chandravanshis in order to settle the dispute and restore the course of the river, but to no avail. The fictional presence of river Saraswati in the story is both an extension of historical records confirming the presence of such a river and a reiteration of the mythopoeic mindset of the ancient Indian storyteller, weaving rich tapestries of orally circulated stories with the magical wand of fantasy. According to Romila Thapar, the river Saraswati, eulogized in the *Rig Veda*, might have originally been the river Hakra or the Ghaggar that had eventually dried up in the Indus basin. "In the *Rig Veda* the geographical focus was the *sapta-sindhu* (the Indus Valley and the Punjab) with *Saraswati* as the sacred river" (2000: 241). The river Saraswati, as Thapar claims in *The Penguin History of Early India*, might have also been the Ghaggar, according to geological sources, that had dried up on account of natural hydraulic changes. But despite doubts about the authenticity of the existence of Saraswati, there are enough historical evidences, as Thapar points out to confirm that the highly sophisticated urban civilization of the Indus system dates back to the third millennium B.C. Hence, the sophisticated ways of life of the Meluhans as conceived by Amish, are not altogether unimaginable. However, there were still many groups of 'tribal societies' that were relatively 'uncivilised' according to the norms of the Meluhans that remained on the peripheries of Devagiri in the novel. The Pakratis who fought with the Gunas and the Nagas are some such tribes that were still not attuned to civilized ways of life, and were hence marginalized by the Meluhans. Romila Thapar observes:

> It is possible that descriptions of those outside the pale of caste society—such as the Shabaras or even the demonic figures said to inhabit the forest, against whom the heroes of the epics had to fight—could be exaggerated accounts of such forest dwellers resisting intruders. The rakshasas of the texts were projected as supernatural beings, and, as part of the unknown wilderness, some were also demonized forest-dwellers. . . . The presentation of forest dwellers as demonic would have emphasized their being alien to caste society. The Shabaras, Pulindas and Nishadas and so on, frequently mentioned in early texts, would have been the prototype. The conventional description is that they were stocky in build, dark in complexion, with bloodshot eyes and speaking a strange language. (56)

The demonizing of the Nagas in Amish's tale almost nearly matches with Thapar's conceptualization and reconstruction of the social and cultural history of ancient India. Among the other features of the novel that lend a 'magical' quality to it as described by Amit Chaudhuri, are the myths and legends from the oral and written literatures of a past that are too remote to be labelled 'historical.' The Puranas provide the major thrust to

Amish's novel, particularly the *Shiva Purana* that weaves the story of Shiva and Sati, and Sati's self-immolation. But Amish tells his own story, choosing to make what Ashis Nandy would have called independent interventions in myths, for myths are "amenable to intervention" (56), lending themselves to interpretations, interpolations and changes in the course of time, unlike history. There might be one more reason behind Amish's choice of the Puranas, for there is a particular school of belief that claims that the Indus Valley civilization was a Vedic civilization, essentially on the basis of evidences from the Puranas. A.N. Chandra in *The Rig-Vedic Culture and the Indus Civilisation* observes:

> Since the majority of the people of this part of the world belonged to the eastern branch of the Mediterranean race from about the 9th or 10th millennium B.C, the people of the Indus cities also belonged to the same race, as also the Vedic Indians. . . . The Indus people belonged to one of the Vedic tribes or 'Janas' and were essentially Indians with Vedic culture. (218)

In the *Shiva Purana*, Sati goes to Daksha's ritual to immolate herself in the sacrificial fire because she is offended by Daksha's insult to Shiva by not inviting him for the fire-yajna. But in Amish's story, Shiva is an invitee who is a detached observer of the ritual organized by Jhooleshwar, the governor of Karachapa. Sati plans to take part in the *agnipariksha* in order to absolve herself of the burden of being an outcast. One has to read the story to get to the core of the details. The blue throat of Shiva, for which he becomes the demi-god Neelkanth, out to save the Meluhans from destruction, is also a variation of the grand narrative of the Puranas, transforming the legendary Shiva of Amish's novel as the rightful incarnation of one of the trinities of Hindu mythology, Mahadeva or Lord Rudra who had swallowed gall in order to protect the gods during the *samudra-manthan*, or 'the Righteous War against the Asuras.' Frequent references to Lord Manu, and his posterity comprising the Suryavanshis and Chandravanshis have also been drawn from the Puranas, namely the genealogical chapter of the *Vishnu Purana* beginning with the seven Manus who claim descent from the Gods. According to Romila Thapar in her essay "Clan, Caste and Origin Myths in Early India," this is primarily a creation myth which speaks of the great flood during the period of the seventh Manu. Manu's children became the ancestors to what is described as the succession of 'rajas' also referred to as the Kshatriyas.

> There are two major descent groups, the Suryavamsa and the Candravamsa. The Suryavamsa is said to have descended from the eldest son of Manu, Iksvaku. . . . The Chandravamsa claims its ancestry from the female half of the androgynous Ila and is therefore also referred to as the Aila Vams. (Thapar 787)

A story crafted in the twenty-first century, replete with a strange fusion of history and myth, as has been mentioned earlier in this study, is not new to Indian English fiction. But what is interesting to note, is the recurrence of the trend of late, particularly in the bestsellers. Ashok K. Banker, another addition to the list of fiction writers in English mentioned in the beginning of the present essay, has made it his mission to rewrite the episodes of the *Ramayana* once again in lucid English meant for the common reader of fiction in India. Investigations into the causes behind the renewed interest in rewriting myths may draw us closer to a theory proposed by Fredric Jameson, one of the best known and controversial cultural critics of the twentieth century, and also one who is crucial to our understanding of contemporary literature and cultural studies. The theory proposed by Jameson relevant to the present study concerns fiction in the "third world countries," a descriptive categorization much maligned by the postcolonial critic Aijaz Ahmad who claims that Jameson's categorization of "third world literature" is pejorative, homogenizing and hence flawed, ignoring the immense heterogeneity of the literary output of those countries listed within the "third world." But what shines through in his argument is a "sweeping hypothesis" as admitted by Jameson himself, which cuts deep into a possible theorization of such novels that use myth and history as their muses. Jameson observes in his essay "Third World Literature in the Era of Multinational Capitalism" published in 1986:

> All third-world texts are necessarily, I want to argue, allegorical, and in a very specific way: they are to be read as what I will call *national allegories*, even when, or perhaps I should say, particularly when their forms develop out of predominantly western machineries of representation, such as the novel. (69)

Jameson further observes:

> Third-world texts, even those which are seemingly private and invested with a properly libidinal dynamic—necessarily project a political dimension in the form of national allegory: *the story of the private individual destiny is always an allegory of the embattled situation of the public third-world culture and society*. (69)

The gross oversimplification of Indian English fiction as *national allegories*, sweepingly hypothetical as it may appear, nevertheless provides vital clues to the analysis of those works of fiction at least, that use as their foundations, mythologies of the past. The clues gain further clarity in the light of the following statements of Jameson from the same essay, "Our traditional concept of allegory—based, for instance, on stereotypes of Bunyan—is that of an elaborate set of figures and personifications to be read against some one-to-one table of equivalences: this is, so to speak, a one-dimensional view of the signifying process" (73). But such equivalences, as Jameson admits, are subject to constant change and transformation at "each perpetual present of the text" (73). It remains to be interrogated, how in the light of Jameson's argument, *The Immortals of Meluha*, and other such works of fiction based on ancient Indian mythology, may be read as national allegories, locked in a life and death struggle with the first world cultural imperialism. We may examine whether narratives such as these are pregnant with the possibilities of creating a counter discourse of national identity through a translation of ancient Indian myths into the language of modern India. Myths as Ashis Nandy has already confirmed are amenable to intervention, and hence are also open to interpretation and re-telling. Nearly two hundred years of colonization has resulted in many erasures. Re-telling myths through fictional constructs may aid in the reconstitutions of the past, as has been engaged upon by writers such as Amish. One may detect allegorical overtones in the struggle of the Meluhans to assert their supremacy over the alien Chandravanshis, particularly in their sense of pride in their past. In Chapter 8 of the novel when Shiva visits Mount Mandar to be witness to the manufacture of the Somras, the elixir of the Meluhans, Brahaspati, the "chief scientist of the empire" takes him around the manufacturing cell. Brahaspati explains to him how the Somras, invented by Lord Brahma after a lot of research, has a magical effect on the aging process, acting as, what he calls an anti-oxidant. The chief scientist in his eulogizing of the Meluhan past, affirms the scientific heritage of the civilization, and hence their superiority over other races. Allegorically perhaps, in the format of popular fiction, Amish's Meluhan myth affirms that science belonged to the East long before the European enlightenment. Brahaspati affirms as the chief scientist of Meluha, "I believe in science. It provides a solution and rationale for everything. And if there is anything that appears like a miracle, the only explanation is that a scientific reason for it has not been discovered as yet" (154). Standing on the brink of a potential extermination threat in the wake of repeated attempts of external aggression, the Pandit of the city of Mohan Jo Daro in Chapter 14 observes, "Civilisation is very fragile. All it takes is a few decades of chaos for us to forget humanity and turn into animals. Our base natures can take over very fast. We can forget that we are sentient beings, with laws and codes and ethics" (231). The supremacy of the Meluhan civilization standing at the crossroads of culture amidst potential threats of devastation from unfriendly neighbours who have not been able to achieve the civilisational norms of perfection, may elicit several allegorical readings, however discontinuous they may seem. The historian and anthropologist in Amish through his fiction almost proves

Aijaz Ahmad wrong that 'national allegories' may still be possible after all in postcolonial Indian-English fiction through the use of myth. Ashis Nandy observes, "myths . . . allow one accesses to the processes which constitute history at the level of the here-and-the-now" (59). He further acknowledges the fact that "myths widen human choices . . . by resisting co-optation by the uniformizing world view of modern science . . . both the science of myth and the scientific status of the myth continue to be a predominantly modern concern" (59). In the light of views of Ashis Nandy, thus, affirmation of the past in Indian English fiction is thus an affirmation of the dignity and autonomy of the so-called "non-modern peoples." 'Modernity' deserves a different theoretical discourse and space, and may be the subject matter of a different essay altogether, but Ashis Nandy's reading of the status of myth in Indian culture facilitates our acceptance and interrogation of the wealth of Indian English novels based on various versions of Indian mythology.

Works Cited

Chaudhuri, Amit. "Huge Baggy Monster: Mimetic Theories of the Indian Novel after Rushdie" *Clearing a Space: Reflections on India, Literature and Culture*. New Delhi: Black Kite, 2008.

Chandra, A.N. *The Rig-Vedic Culture and the Indus Civilization*. Calcutta: Ratna Prakashan, 1980.

Jameson, Frederic. "Third World Literature in the Era of Multinational Capitalism," *Social Text*, No 15 (Autumn 1986): 65-68. *JSTOR*, 23 June 2011.

Nandy, Ashis. *The Intimate Enemy: Loss and Recovery of Self under Colonialism*. New Delhi: Oxford University Press, 1983.

Thapar, Romila. *The Penguin History of Early India*. New Delhi: Penguin, 2002.

_____. *Cultural Pasts: Essays in Early Indian History*. New Delhi: Oxford University Press, 2000.

Tripathy, Amish. *The Immortals of Meluha: Book 1 of the Shiva Trilogy*. Chennai: Westland, 2010.

Shashi Tharoor's *The Great Indian Novel*: A Study in Narrative

RAMA CHOWDHURY

Shashi Tharoor's The Great Indian Novel, *published in 1989, is an exquisite political satire and a mock-heroic narrative in prose. In fact it is so many other things at once. It is the fictionalised account of India's Independence Movement and the political events of the first 3 decades of Free, Democratic India. So it is history as well; history of the birth, rise, running, split and temporary loss of the National Congress Party of India. But what seems to be the most striking about the book is not the content of the story but the way of telling it.*

The extraordinary narrative takes us for a jolly tour through the panorama of events and people that shaped the fate of our nation. The lofty epic framework of the Mahabharata *is brilliantly used to relate the political story of a nation.* The Great Indian Novel *transforms the family saga of Kauravas and Pandavas into a modern saga of India's most significant historical period. The narrative is such an amazing fusion of history and epic, of lofty truths and shameful realities, of facts and fantasies that one is baited to go through it again and again in search of its various dimensions. The narrator entertains us with abundant puns, allusions, wit and satire which transcend the facts into a fabulous tale. At the same time the narrative has such strength as to make one look back both at our history and our grand epic. Myth and reality collide with each other in course of it and render it a grand piece of retrospect, revelation, reversal and retrieval.*

Indian English fiction writing of 80s and 90s marked a remarkable shift from the novels of frustration, doubt and disenchantment of earlier decades and found a plural, cynical, self-assessing and even self-asserting voice at the face of the Western unitary sets of ontology and epistemology. Salman Rushdie's *Midnight's Children* was undoubtedly the distinct torch bearer in this penetrating and cynical tradition of looking at history as well as contemporary time of our great nation. The diverse and sometimes contrasting layers of Indian reality have frequently suffered biased and inadequate treatment at the hands of many Western and indigenous writers/historians. Writers like Rushdie, Arundhati Roy, and Shashi Tharoor etc. tried and succeeded in presenting that Indian identity of multiple layers by amalgamating personal elements with social, historical and political elements, by marrying off myth and reality, satire and self-assessment, past and present.

Tharoor's *The Great Indian Novel* (1989) belongs to the above-mentioned category of Indian English fiction. It hails such an irreverent, iconoclastic and hilariously satirical tone that entertains the audience as well as provokes them to think. Tharoor here attempts to catch the glimpses of pre- and post-Independence India in terms of its multiplicities and seeks resorts to a narrative pattern befitting his attempt. the *Mahabharata*, our greatest epic of never-ending storehouse of myths, events, stories, characters, narrative patterns, allegories, morals, political and religious ideologies etc. is held by Tharoor as his literary ideal. He presents the relatively modern political history of India clad in the colourful mythical and allegorical robe of the *Mahabharata.*

The narrative of *The Great Indian Novel* takes us for a jolly tour through the panorama of events and people that shaped the fate of our nation. The epic structure of the *Mahabharata* has deftly been used to relate the generational progress of Indian politics starting from colonialism to nationalism and therefrom to post-Independence era reaching 1980s. The major events and characters of the *Mahabharata* find their counterparts in the major events and leaders of Indian politics. Myths and legends are retained, recreated, relived, reconstructed and sometimes even destroyed in the course of the colourful narrative of *The Great Indian Novel.*

What could have been a mere historical record of modern India, has turned out to be a thoroughly enjoyable literary piece as Tharoor opts for a brilliant narrative style with so many dimensions. The rendering of the facts of recent India into the epic stature of the *Mahabharata* is both hilarious and impressive. No other narrative pattern could have justified the story of our great nation which has as much variety and significance as the great epic itself. In writing *The Great Indian Novel* Tharoor adopts the external framework of the *Mahabharata,* namely dividing his book into 18 chapters. Most of the fictionalised characters and names in Tharoor's book bear identical resemblance with those of *The Mahabharata.* At the same time the author shows uniqueness in relating the major happenings of Indian history through the mouth of the extraordinarily witty and self-conscious VVji.

It is important that from the very beginning Tharoor is consciously out to create a narrative discourse of our own. He is well aware of the common trends and often biasness of presenting history. But for a nation as ours, it is not an easy task to find a suitable mode or pattern to narrate its history. The uncountable people and events of our National Movement with their various shades and shadows, the inseparable magic and mania attached to them from the beginning to the present time, the age-old cultural tradition and values of innumerable diversities—all these demand an essentially competent narrative to justify them. Tharoor employs his utmost capability to do so in *The Great Indian Novel.*

The first recognizable characteristic of Tharoor's narrative is its openness and mobility. Unlike a static, historical account of facts, his story runs as a living creature. Time, space, place and people are dealt with in their multiplicities. Legends and myths are bared at one point, on the next facts are clad in many layers of myths or magic. The whole narrative vibrates with the cantankerous narrator's (VVji) unparallel liking for pun, humour, satire and a wide and varied range of allusions. He takes liberty of digressing whenever he finds a thing to ponder at and claims irrelevances as his right in narrating India's very own story. VVji tells 'amanuensis' Ganapathi, "put it all down. Every word I say. We're not writing a piddling Western thriller here. This is my story, the story of Ved Vyas, eighty-eight years old. And full of irrelevancies, but it could become nothing less than the Great Indian Novel." (18).

As told earlier, the narrative design of *The Great Indian Novel* chiefly retains the grand epic design of the *Mahabharata* in structure, in characterisation and in narrative technique. The Hastinapur saga of Pandavas and Kauravas is adapted to relate the saga of birth, rise, ruling, temporary loss and regaining power of the National Congress Party of India. The 18 chapters in the fiction, like their epic equivalents, choose a significant event or person to focus on. However, the first 6 chapters hold Ganga Datta at the centre. He is the Vishma or Devabrata of the *Mahabharata* and he is also our legendary leader Gandhiji. The first few important moves by our greatest leader set the wheel of national movement on pace. Tharoor does not deny his role or his impact but at the same time nor does he stop to locate and ridicule at his obsession with experimentation of truth, chastity etc. Such apparently innocent observation from VVji's part will testify to this: "Ganga D. would always have a penchant for making his most dramatic gestures before a sizable audience. One day he was even to die in front of a crowd." (23)

Keeping with the original story *The Great Indian Novel* traces the life and career of the descendents of king Shantanu. Ganga D. takes one mission after another like Bugebuge factory workers' cause, (Jute Mill Workers's Wage Reformation), Motihari Peasants Resistance (Chaurichaura Indigo Farmers' Cause) and the historical Mango March (Dandi March) etc. with a huge number of followers. At the same time the family tree flourishes with the birth and growing up of the blind Dhritarashtra (the idealistic and blindly visionary Jawaharlal Nehru), the pale Pandu (the hot and hectic Netaji) and the wise Bidur (Sardar Vallabhbhai Patel). India's freedom movement with its ups and downs had direct bearing on the personal life of these leaders. Tharoor makes their stories highly entertaining with lots of anecdotes while at intervals the poking continues at the mishaps and mistakes done by these leaders in the name of patriotism, idealism etc.

Myths and memories overlap each other as the brooding old narrator talks of Mahammad Ali Karna, the man behind Karnistan (Jinnah and the Formation of Pakistan). The *Mahabharata's* character of Karna finds a unique equivalent in the character of Mahammad Ali Jinnah. Congress Party suffered from more than one fissure at that time and the nation watched its gruesome communal riots all over the country. However, in the midst of chaos and confusion Independence was achieved and Gangaji being killed, the power politics took new dimensions. The narrator here grows bolder as he recounts more complex game of power and politics. The action in the *Mahabharata* culminates in the Great War at Kurukshetra. The event encases so many dramatic stunts, laudable heroism, shameful betrayal, shocking reversals and finally sings the win of Dharma or the Good over the Adharma or Evil. Tharoor's version of that great war in modern India is also the most crucial political scenario of Independent India during the period of Indira Gandhi as prime minister.

On one side there is Priya Duryudhani, the vicious, determined power monger who alone equals a hundred sons supposed to be born to her parents. On the other side there are five Pandavas: 1) Yudhisthir who stands for harmless and practically ineffective Indian Judiciary system. Also recognizable in him is the honest but powerless fourth prime minister Morarji Desai. 2) Bhim is the strongest Pandava who represents Indian Army immune to any corruption (till then). 3) Arjun is the Indian News Media. 4) & 5) Nakul & Sahadev are Indian Civil Service and Indian Foreign Service. This seems to be the most challenging part of Tharoor's narrative as the many shades of characters and events of this period are capable of bamboozling anyone. Of course, he too employs more than one mode of narration like prose, poetry, legends, myths, folktales etc. to meet the demand. The stories and legends of Eklavya (The role played by V.V. Giri and Fakhruddin Ali Ahmed), Ashwathama (Jagjibon Ram), Shikhandi (Nathuram Binayak Godse) and many more are skilfully woven into the texture of Tharoor's 'song of modern India.' And every myth or legend or even character that Tharoor introduces in course of his narrative has more than one shade in them. Our cultural as well as political multiplicities are hailed by the author as our true identity.

Independent India's march with major events like accession of royal states, war with Pakistan and China, division of National Congress party, creation of Bangladesh, rise of Janata Party, the (in)famous declaration of emergency, defeat of Indira etc. are dealt with hilarious humour and pricking punch. To suspend our disbelief, besides facts and records, the omniscient narrator takes resorts to dream, eavesdropping and of course, sheer imagination in giving an animated account of Indian history. Draupadi Mokrasi or D. Mokrasi's (read Democracy) plight at the hands of autocratic Priya Duryudhani and other coincidences led the modern Pandavas, under the leadership of Drona (read Jayaprakash Narayan), to stand against the repression and enjoy a temporary win. The narrative takes a seemingly abrupt end though for that too VVji has his clarifications. "What remains to be said, Ganapathi? There is, of course, the question of expectations, yours as much as our characters.' There is no story and too many stories; there are no heroes and too many heroes. What is left out matters almost as what is said." (411)

The narrative of *The Great Indian Novel* is certainly a retelling of India's colonial past and the successive post-Independent political history of India from a reverse perspective. The British colonialists are painted stereotypes and such caricaturing seems to be a deliberate on Tharoor's part as an apt retort and parody to the depiction of caricature-like Indians by Western writers in books like *A Passage to India* or in pages of Kipling's books. Satire, wit, a tongue-in-cheek humour and an exquisite free play with rhetoric devices as pun, allusion, metaphor etc. characterise the whole narrative to our great delight while the ponderous political veteran-turned narrator evokes so many questions in us about our past and present. The blend of wit and humour, of knowledge and long-time-lulled emotions of the narrative reminds one of the excellences of the Metaphysical poets.

The wide range of allusions in the book is a world in themselves. Starting from the title 'The Great Indian Novel' to the titles of 18 chapters in the book alludes to our ancient texts and works of both foreign and native writers of much relevance. Paul Scott's *The Jewel in the Crown* (The Duel with the Crown—2nd Book), Louis Bromfield's *The Rains Came* (The Rains Came—3rd Book), Scott's *Raj Quartet* (A Raj Quartet 4th Book), again Scott's *The Towers of Silence* (The Powers of Silence—5th Book), Hemingway's *The Sun also Rises* (The Son Also Rises—7th Book), Rushdie's *Midnight's Children* (*Midnight's Parents* 8th Book), Kipling's *Kim* (9th Book), *The Man Who Would be King* (12th Book), *Jungle Book* (16th Book), Arthur Koestler's *Darkness at Noon etc.* are some of the books being alluded to in Tharoor's narrative. Names such as Heaslop, Bibigarh etc. are also recognised having reference to books written by Westerners on India, though in a parodical manner. Heaslop is a character in Forster's *A Passage to India* while Bibigarh is the prominent backdrop in *The Jewel in the Crown.*

Innumerable puns with which Tharoor dots his writing are interesting in their novelty. With the name of places like Karnistan, the hacked off country (Pakistan), La'slut' (La'hore'), Comea (Goa), Gelabin (Bengal), Manimir (Money or Mani as counterpart of cash (Kashmir), Chakra (China), Snoop-ing (Peking-peek-ing) etc., with names of persons and parties like Gangaji (Gandhiji), Zaleel Shah Jhoota (Zulfikar Ali Bhutto), D. Mokrasi (Democracy), People's Front (Janata Party), Onward Organisation (All India Forward Block) etc. are but a few examples from the pun-prone book. Tharoor's innovations are amusing and at the same time the satirical note is quite recognisable.

Tharoor or rather the much-experienced VVji does not care much to keep a distinct borderline between myth and reality, between fact and fiction as they are essentially inseparable in the present context. So we listen to an old storyteller who often lcavcs his storics without an cnd, or at lcast without any logical end. The tone of irreverence and mockery in giving account of our great leaders' foolish, crazy deeds may invite anger and rage in many readers. But the narrative itself defends and justifies the necessity of it. The mock-heroic approach acts both as a shield and a weapon. The mythical rendering of modern history distances and diminishes the harshness of some of our crudest facts of history. On the other hand, the satirical tone enables the narrative to create a discourse of doubt and also disillusionment. Some of the dearly-lulled sublime images were ripped of their glory and glamour and the revelations are sometimes shocking.

The dominant concern in *The Great Indian Novel* is politics, that too national politics. But as other socio-cultural aspects are not independent of politics, they come and mingle with the main aspect spontaneously. Brahmins, the privileged class in Hindu caste system, are depicted with touch of irony. "Our Brahmins got about a lot in those days . . . and they didn't need any hotel bookings then. . . . He would be offered his host's hospitality, his food, his bed and often, because there were a lot more understanding then, his daughter as well." (19)

By casting our national history and heroes in the structure and characters of the great epic, Tharoor is able to reflect on the socio-political tradition of India in general. The self-conscious narrator never misses the opportunity to defend the omissions or distortions in his narrative. Ganapathi and also the readers are told: "That for every tale I have told you, every perception I have conveyed, there are a hundred equally valid alternatives I have omitted." (373)

Ganapathi, whom the octogenarian narrator appoints as his 'amanuensis,' also represents the readers who are supposed to go through this amusingly political satire. At intervals VVji keeps on giving clarifications before Ganapathi, assuming the latter's doubt or disbelief in his version of the story. He is well aware of the difference of opinion existing among the politicians, historians and also the commoners regarding the people and events he is narrating here. So he often begs excuses for digressions, distortions and at the same time defends imagination as the most befitting instrument to relate the multi-layered political history of a vast nation. Because, a static and prosaic account of the same would have deprived us of the magic and myth which are now but integral part of our culture.

The book ends on a rather preacher-like tone of VVji, his reigning verbal wit being absent towards the end. The discourse of doubt, questioning and baring of truth now casts its light on vision also. What lie before us are the words of Dharma to Yudishtir: "Accept doubt and diversity. . . . Reject equally the sterility of ideologies and the passionate prescriptions of those who think themselves infallible. . . . Admit that there is more than one truth, more than one Right, more than one dharma." (418) The book ends but not the story as VVji puts it, "stories never end, they just continue somewhere else."

Works Cited

Said, Edward. *Orientalism: Western Conception of the Orient*. Penguin, New Delhi, 1992.

Spivak, Gayatri. *In Other Worlds: Essays in Cultural Politics*. Methuen, New York, 1987.

Culler, Jonathan. 'Making History: The Power of Narrative.' *Narrative: A Seminar*, ed. Amiya Dev. Sahitya Akademi, Delhi, 1994.

Sharma, Meenakshi. 'Narrating Indian History in Fiction from an Indigenous Perspective: Shashi Tharoor's *The Great Indian Novel*.' *Native Responses to Contemporary Indian English Novel*, ed. Rangarao Bhongle. Atlantic, New Delhi, 2003.

Tharoor, Shashi. *The Great Indian Novel*. Penguin, New Delhi, 1989.

Raj Kamal Jha's *The Blue Bedspread: A Psychoanalytical Study*

C.L. KHATRI

The present age is the age of novel following unprecedented boom in the field of novel. Consequently new novel writers are coming up regularly on the scene with an eye on the market and fingers on the nerves of the target readers. They are well received by the media as well as readers. Indian writers in English have been cashing in upon this opportunity. It is in this context that I am taking up a new emerging novelist, Raj Kamal Jha who hails from Bihar. Jha, a journalist by profession, made his appearance felt with his first novel The Blue Bedspread *published in 1999. It won for him the Commonwealth Writers' Award for Best First Book. It was also shortlisted for the Guardian Book Award and named as a New York Times Notable Book of the year. The present study is an attempt to evaluate and explore the thematic and artistic aspects of his novel more so from a psychoanalytical perspective than a socio-cultural perspective since it is a character-oriented novel. It requires a critic to delve deep into the psyche of his characters who make a bold and audacious confession of incest, sodomy, promiscuous sojourn and a blazing account of Id's pleasure principle and ego's intervention at a matured stage of life to unravel the dark secrets of the past and get rid of its ghost, the guilt consciousness.*

Raj Kamal Jha was born in 1966 at Karmauli in Madhubani district of Bihar. He had his education in Kolkata where he spent his first eighteen years before coming over to New Delhi. Currently he is working as the executive editor of *The Indian Express*. Jha is a Mechanical engineering graduate and has a Master's degree in journalism from the University of Southern California, Los Angeles, U.S.A. He has so far produced two novels *The Blue Bedspread* (1999) and *If You Are Afraid of Heights* (2003) from Picador, England. Both these books are dedicated to his mother Rajana Jha and his father Munishwar Jha. His father was a distinguished Professor of Hindi in Calcutta University, Calcutta. His first novel *The Blue Bedspread* won the Commonwealth Writers' Award for Best First Book. It was short listed for the Guardian Book Award and named as a New York Times Notable Book of the Year.

The present study is an attempt to evaluate and explore the thematic and artistic aspects of his novel more so from a psycho-analytical perspective than a socio-cultural perspective. His first novel *The Blue Bedspread* has created ripples in the ocean of fiction by making a bold and audacious confession of incest, sodomy, promiscuous sojourn and a blazing account of Id's pleasure principle and ego's intervention at a matured stage of life to unravel the dark secrets of the past and get rid of its ghost, the guilt consciousness, "he doesn't have to lie any more, twist facts to flesh out his fiction." (227) The Biblical power of confession and the final assertion of truth however unpalatable bring a re-affirmation of strength and a revalidation of joy. It was well appreciated by critics abroad and by a few in India as well. It was not as lavishly praised in India as it was done by critics abroad. John Fowles calls it "Something rather remarkable, almost a coming of age of the Indian novel." (Blurb) Ophelia Field writes in the *Times Literary Supplement*, "Raj Kamal Jha knows how to take us by the scruff of our clichés, lead us down seemingly predictable paths and then swerve sharply sideways." Whereas M.K. Naik takes an objective stand while appreciating it: "*The Blue Bedspread,* like *A Short History of Everything,* is 'a memory novel,' but here the memories of the narrator are sadder and even more sordid. They include being abused by a drunken father, and an uncomfortable, incestuous relationship with his sister. The 'Blue Bedspread' in the title becomes a symbol of escape into a more pleasant world of imagination for both the children. Raj Kamal Jha's evocation of the past is far more sensitively done than Bhatia's, but the attitude of his protagonist to his abnormal experience remains intriguingly ambivalent, raising suspicions of masochism." (72)

Namita Gokhale has all praise for it: "*The Blue Bedspread* is important because it is authentic in its voice, in its depiction of the internal sensibility of a culture that is enervated, exhausted, driven by pain and despair and joylessness to the very edge." (*The Hindu*)

I don't believe that Indian culture has come to that state which is projected, if the bizarre setting is taken as a sample for generalization of culture as Namita Gokhale takes the case. Again I don't understand how "it is coming of age of the Indian novel." If one looks at it from a socio-cultural perspective, one will come to the same conclusion that R.B. Singh arrives at in his paper "*The Blue Bedspread*: Spreading Incest":

> As a case of incest, it is only too unpalatable and never a common general phenomenon. As an ideal familial bond between brother and sister it does not stand its ground as the sister elopes with her lover without telling her brother. As such, thematically it portrays a malignant tumour of our too busy life in an age which advances progressively backwards. The author creates a bizarre setting in which sexual aberration is a rule rather than the exception. No wonder, Father beats his wife and daughter, sodomizes his son. Mother waves to her lover, sister sleeps with his brother. . . . All too bizarre, sickening and nauseating! (175-76)

The Blue Bedspread is a psychological novel in the sense that it exploits the stream-of-consciousness technique to convert the narrative of outer action into a drama of the life of the mind. The time span of the novel is just one and half day. An unexpected event at midnight in the life of the narrator sets in the thought process going back through the dark tunnel of his memory. The narrative begins with a telephone call at midnight to the protagonist, the narrator, who lives in a rented flat of two rooms in Calcutta. The police officer informs him that his sister has died in labour leaving behind a baby girl. The question "Do you know who the father is?" sets him reeling in retrogressive thought process. He is lost in the old days of intimacy spent together with his sister. He does not answer the question. He is in the state of quandary and indecision whether he should adopt the child or not. The response is unbecoming of an Indian brother. An Indian brother would normally be prompt in accepting the newborn baby of his deceased sister. However, he goes to the hospital and brings in his sister's baby wrapped in a blue towel. He puts her in his bedroom on the blue bedspread and addressing her he relates the multicoloured episodes of his past life and projects the future of the baby in the same breath. Soon he overcomes his inhibition and pours on her all the love and care he can; 'And I shall hold the spoon close to my chest so that if you wish to, you can imagine I'm your mother and the milk flows, drop by drop, from her breast.' (183)

So the character is intriguingly ambivalent in his attitude to the stories he is going to tell her. But he is evasive of the truth about the baby's origin: "In short, I will tell you happy stories and I will tell you sad stories. And remember, my child, your truth lies somewhere in between." (6) He identifies the baby with his sister in sleep, "when she slept, it was as if she had walked into a photograph." (23) He goes deep into its root and discovers the reason in her recurrent dream in which she sees a painter making a painting of her on the canvas and he asks her not to move. Dream is an important device in Jha's narrative art in both novels.

The novel is neatly divided into five sections: Father, Mother, Sister, Visitors and Brother. They are the main characters and Jha has taken care of the seniority. The brother being the youngest comes in the last. But the narrative revolves round him and his rare intimacy with his sister. We don't have much information about his father. The reader only knows that he is a habitual drinker who often beats his wife and daughter; and he does stupid things when he is drunk. Once he flushes a kitchen knife down the toilet and it remains blocked for two days. Consequently both brother and sister are forced to hold back their shit for two days. At other times he hides his daughter's sanitary napkins so that she is forced to borrow her brother's handkerchief. Sometimes he bleeds himself while shaving. At such moments Sister shakes him and even slaps him hard to bring him in conscious state. He eccentrically laughs and sometimes cries. Strangely enough one day he sodomizes his son. He blackmails the boy to lie naked on the blue bedspread saying that he knows what he does with his sister at night everyday. "I closed my eyes, undressed and on Father's orders lay on the blue bedspread" (59). To me what is artistically striking is the pattern of contrast in the background scene and the images—auditory and visual. The stillness of the room is set in contrast with the sound outside as if evoking the sound of the furry must be rising within him:

> It was cold, the rain from the exercise books had seeped into the fabric. I could hear the sound of cars splashing the water in the potholes outside, I could hear the minibus conductors shout their destinations: Dum Dum, Howrah, Entally, Roxy Cinema.
>
> Someone laughed from the street outside; I think I shouted, I'm not sure. Even if I had, my scream wouldn't have gone beyond the places where buses go. (59)

He seems to explore the music of silence, stillness and darkness with the aid of contrasting images as in the bed scene:

> That night, my sister didn't switch on the bedside lamp. And with all the stars locked in the blackness of the bedroom, we held each other tight . . . my chin to rest on the small pillow of her breast and my hands pressed, warm and soft, between her legs.
>
> We could hear Father snore in the next room, the rattle of the windows whenever a huge Bengal-Bihar cargo truck rumbled by . . .

> I lay there awake, staring at the darkness so comfortably nestled between our bodies allowing to wash my eyes, lull me to sleep. And although my body still hurt, where Father had put his entire weight on that evening, I kept drowning in a stream, a river and then an ocean of happiness. (61-62)

The picture of an uncouth and permissive father and an unhappy home reminds one of D.H. Lawrence's own story as the nucleus of *Sons and Lovers*. But it has a philosophy to advocate whereas *The Blue Bedspread* falls flat when we find that sister is maintaining a simultaneous love affair with another person. And she elopes with him at the age of nineteen never to come back. The lover recoils into the boot of brother; and she rationalizes her elopement as a sacrifice for him and as a saving grace. Perhaps it is time that heels the wound:

> And then, slowly, like sunrise on a winter's day, it dawned on me, cold and clear, that perhaps my sister had to run away for me to carry on. Because, in a way, it was essential that one of us should leave never to return. It saved both of us the discomfort and the pain of sitting together as adults and talking about everything except those nights on the blue bedspread, that July night on the blue bedspread, moments that were key to our survival and yet better left untouched and unsaid. (62-63)

However, there is another aspect of the father. He loves his wife and children. He gives his children a rupee every day when they go to school. He takes his son to stammering clinic. And above all he has a sense of guilt and repentance though it is verbally inarticulated but it culminates into his silent departure from the scene. The narrator has reconciled with the situation while his father has not. As the narrator relates:

> On certain rainswept nights, when I lie in bad, I can see father standing in the rain outside, his hair all wet, the water streaming across his face. . . . Instead he looks weak, lost, like a child left stranded in the blinding rain. (63)

He further adds: "But when I look at the window again it's late, father is gone, leaving behind the rain pouring out from a dark Calcutta night." (63)

The image of "dark Calcutta" evokes the darkness and gloominess of his life. It is a device that intensifies the effect. But the protagonist appears passive rather so self-indulgent that he practically does nothing to recover his sister and his father rather imagines to have his own wife and children and wishes for the sister to be safe with her own children. He doesn't even fancy to have her back. The brother undergoes the maturing process. He is later seen as passionate lover, an aphrodite who has got a nymphomaniac medical student as a sex-partner. They first experiment with the recess provided in the park, cinema hall and even the college. Incredible it sounds that one night the girl forcibly takes out her mother's eyes to facilitate her sexual adventure at her own place. This episode reminds one vividly of the common practice going on in the public places in metro cities.

Given the background of a promiscuous brother and perverse father one can safely add that the main plot is based on Freud's Oedipus complex and Electra complex. Their conduct can best be interpreted in a psychoanalytical criticism: "Most of our actions are motivated by psychological forces over which we have very limited control." (127) Freud designates the prime psychic force as libido or the Id and he also says that childhood is a period of intense sexual experience. According to this theory the hero of the novel has reached the stage of genital primacy and Oedipus complex manifests itself when he is around ten years old. Since he has lost his mother, has seen little love of father who is rather insulated, he is naturally drawn to his sister. The lack of space in the two-room flat and the absence of mother compel her to share the same bed with her bother who is younger to her. She naturally looks after her. This physical and psychological intimacy gives ample scope to the Id to play on its pleasure principle. Later on when they grow up fully conscious of the social codes, the ego in them intercepts the Id and they make a hasty retreat. His sister makes love with some one else and runs away. He picks up another sex partner and nurtures the desire of having his own wife and children. However, he fails in it and his beloved refuses to marry him. The novel culminates into a Super ego stage that emboldens him to accept the truth before a vast imaginary audience in the Eden Garden:

> I am tired, I shall quietly remove one pillow and lie down beside you, adjust myself so that your head fits exactly in the curve of my neck. Let us sleep for a while because tonight is the night they will all be there, we shall wake up only when the stadium is full, the microphone is ready, the amplifiers have been tested. For tonight is the Eden Gardens night. (222)

And he declares, "I am the father of my sister's child" in eight long pauses in the last chapter "Eight words." Interestingly this is the only chapter in which the narrator is third person and actor is the first person. This breaking of the sentence takes us back to the fifth chapter in which we come to know that he suffers from stammering disease. So the narrative is not as much a story telling as a recollection of memories aside. It is an inner process. To compensate his speech handicap, his father has trained him at writing. "The most important lesson my father taught me. When you find it difficult to say something, when the words get trapped in your chest, your lips quiver, as in winter, you can always write it down" (35) The ambivalence comes out as a distinct feature of this narrative. It remains intriguing if he is the real father or foster father of the baby even after his declaration. Having reconciled with the past, the protagonist adopts the baby and consoles her in emotionally charged language:

> I need to put your mind to rest, no one's going to take you away. I shall call up Mr. Chatterjee, tell him that he doesn't need to wait any more, the man and the woman will surely find another child somewhere in this city of twelve million.

> So it shall be I who will take you to the Alipore zoo. (221)

It is the art of the narrative that attracts any one more than its story that is very thin and morally disagreeable. The very first section "First Story" gives the effect of workshop novel and establishes a rapport with the reader. He thinks of several options of beginning the narrative: "'I could begin with my name. . . . I could begin with the way." (1) And the beginning is no less thought-provoking than the interpersonal relationship in the novel. The anonymous protagonist-cum-narrator's justification of his going without name at once touches us. "I could begin with my name but forget it, why waste time, it doesn't matter in this city of twelve million names." (1) All main characters, sister, mother and father are nameless as a common man in the city is. It is a realistic picture of city that likes a solitary, nameless, faceless man.

> This city likes lonely people, the city likes this man.
>
> There's no one to walk by his side, to wait for him at a street crossing, soothe city moves in to help, it slows down the traffic, parts the crowds. There's no one to talk to him, so the city speaks through its banners, its hoardings. At night, he has nothing to do, so the streetlights trap insects in their Plexiglas covers, lull him to sleep. (74)

It is an authentic but ironic remark on the city life. It may be an act to identify himself with the masses, to present penetrating and rare shades and tints of their life with the sensitivity of a poet. The main story, however, defies this objective, though it is reflected in many of the episodes like a drunkard father beating his daughter just for a rupee, husband-wife quarrel, a mill getting closed after workers' strike, scenes of Durga puja, maternity ward, bus-ride, tram wire hanging loose in rain, the flooded drains, heap of garbage, open manholes and filthy streets in the rainy season and in the general portrayal of city life. The evocation of Calcutta a musty, bleak and congested city of twelve million people through commonplace images of rain, drain, flood, snowfall etc. is exquisitely drawn. Maya Jaggi rightly believes, "It is this sense of city, with its under tow of violence redeemed by love and imagination that gives the book its grace." (*Guardian*)

The art of narration amply shows the possibility of a brilliant storyteller in Raj Kamal Jha. He employs the baby at one level as a catalytic agent that sets him narrating and writing the story of his sister and many stories and episodes told to him by her sister. He appears time-stricken, because there is a dead line before him. Perhaps this is why he jumbles up several things in one breath:

> There isn't much time, the man and the woman are coming to take you tomorrow, the fire was still burning when we left, let me tell you about the doctor with arms as white as milk. (21)

This quick movement of clauses throws light on his uneasiness and a mental state of running out of time. He is preparing this document to hand it over to the man and the woman who are coming to him in the morning to adopt the baby. So it is aimed at the posterity. He expects them to retell the whole story to her when she grows up. Interestingly he does not think of adopting her himself until he finishes his account. So the oral tradition of story telling and the art of private documentation about the family history work here to recover and regenerate fatherly instinct in him. He realizes the vanity of concocting facts with fiction and garners enough moral strength to walk naked as a baby.

It is the effect of constricting time and space that he repeats the same sentence and expression several times. 'I could begin with my name,' 'I am sorry, sir, your sister is dead.' and some other expressions are repeated more than once.

The novel is remarkable for the adroit use of stream-of-consciousness and the first person narrative technique. The novelist employs the first person narrative technique with an ambivalence of authorial voice and the voice of a leading character, the protagonist. It enables him to present an authentic voice of the exploration of the self, and gives us an inside view of the subconscious and unconscious layers of the protagonist's mind. Since it is predominantly a subjective realm, the choice of technique is appropriate. Jha adopts a third person narrator in his second novel *If You Are Afraid of Height* to suit its theme. The narrator drifts along the stream of his consciousness. Since late at night until next day except the narrator's cremating his sister and bringing her baby home from the hospital, there is no other action in the present. The rest of the novel contains the narrator's recollection of his past and his version of the future for the baby. Naturally in the stream of the mind, time gets intermingled. Past, present and future forfeit their sequence in that stream. At one and the same moment the narrator's consciousness of the present is intercepted by the past and led into the future.

The narrative is episodic apparently inorganic and episodes unravel themselves through the mind of the narrator. The sequence of time and subject is frequently fractured but the different episodes of life are put into an organic structure of the novel giving us a feel of the collage of life. The novel begins with the question "Do you know who the father is?" and ends with the answer spoken in eight words with long pauses after each word in a highly dramatic fashion, 'I-am-the-father-of-my-sister's-child.' The image of the "blue bedspread" and 'the child lying' also help in giving an organic structure to the novel. The "blue bedspread" is a symbol of the earth as well as the blue heaven for the brother and the sister:

> There are smells in our garden. The earth is the blanket, musty and warm; the grass is our clothes, smelling of water and shop and sun, the blue bedspread is the night, the flowers are my sister's shampoo, the wind is the breath of approaching sleep. (109-10)

Later on when he is left alone and a new girl comes in his life, he replaces the blue bedspread with a new bed sheet 'Black with a giant white conch shell drawn in the centre and tiny white conch shells all around the four sides of its rectangle' (195). It certainly points to the subtle symbolic symmetry of the novel. In a black bed sheet there is a white conch. He doesn't want to meddle with the two affairs and he attaches a distinct value to his relationship with his sister. 'White conch' is a symbol of love and life amidst gloom and darkness that envelopes the protagonist. However, the blue bedspread reappears for the baby with same image of light and stars.

> So that the light falls in a million specks on the blue bedspread making our sky shimmer with stars. And let me lean over you and spin the shade so that the stars move in orbits across the bed, over your body, your fingers, across the two pillows, which serve as your walls, in the hollows where my fingers were. (221)

The novel on the whole is neatly crafted, simple in its structure, soft and poetic in its language, rich in images of visuals, sound and colours; and offers a subtle account of a character's psyche or a juvenile's intense sexual enterprise prompted by prime psychic force as well as their circumstances in the house. The case of incest as it is presented here is by no means intentional or motivated however resonating its flavour maybe in his later days.

Works Cited

Naik, M.K. *Indian English Literature 1980-2000: A Critical Survey*, New Delhi: Pencraft International, 2001.

Jha, Raj Kamal. *The Blue Bedspread*, London: Picador, 2000.

R.B. Singh. "*The Blue Bedspread*: *Spreading Incest*," *Indian Writing in English: Voices from the Oblivion*, ed. C.L. Khatri. Jaipur: Book Enclave, 2004.

Qtd. Wilfred L. Guerin et al. *A Handbook of Critical Approaches to Literature* O.U.P: Oxford, 1999

Makarand Paranjape's *The Narrator: A Novel*: A Psychoanalytical Study

TAMOJOY BRAHMA

Of all the genres of Indian English literature, fiction is the most developed and well received one in the postmodern period both at home and abroad. Indian English fiction has brought a revolution in the whole range of Indian English literature in the choice of subjects and language of expression. And Makarand Paranjape's debut novel The Narrator: A Novel *(1995) is a timely and necessary rejoinder to the communities of writer and readers located in India that attempts the postmodern narrativity in a refreshingly new way. The central concern of the novel is to represent a potential writer's anxiety about the making of a narrative or a novel. Rahul Patwardhan, the protagonist, a Lecturer of English at Asafia University, Hyderabad embodies the anxiety of arriving as a writer. And a work of art, according to the Freudian paradigm, is a disguised fulfillment of a suppressed or repressed sexual wish. Hence the paper attempts to analyze Paranjape's novel in the light of psychoanalytic criticism within the framework of the main ideas of Sigmund Freud and Jacques Lacan. It shows how Rahul's disease-creative schizophrenia shatters him into three parts—Rahul: Baddy: Badri—and how his aspirations are tied up with Lacanian notions about Lack, Gap, Desire (for the Other), and movement from the Imaginary to the Symbolic Order. The paper also analyses the character of Rahul while taking into considerations the Freudian model of Id, Ego and Super-ego. The special ability of the artist to shift the original libidinal drives from their sexual orientations to non-sexual higher goal—a "fantasized wish-fulfillment" through the creation of a Bollywoodian script* Manpasand—*is also dealt with in the paper. It also highlights the Deleuze and Félix Guattarian models of the schizoanalysis—that "schizophrenia" embraces "a positive process"—a rhetorical trope to write a fiction. Hence by the end of the narrative, the protago-*

nist Rahul and his creator, Paranjape's "very desiree of a novel" is fulfilled—the manifesto of a writer anxious to arrive as a novelist is satisfied.

> *There are, no doubt, many different types of the novel, each with its own strengths and weaknesses, advantages and drawbacks, peaks and pitfalls. But the novel I want to write is intelligent in form, self-conscious in technique. It entertains without being superficial, moves without being boring and priggish. It has a serious soul, yet is light-hearted. It has a stunning figure and mysterious depths. Its face is serious, striking, even noble, but it also has a hint of a smile on its lips. Innovative, even brash in telling, carefree and slightly flirtatious in manner, it has a sense of allure to it, a degree of suspense which tickles the observers' curiosity. It may even be somewhat risqué—naughty, teasing, arousing; it wears a tint of the erotic, like lipstick or blush, without drawing undue attention to itself. In a word, a novel born of jouissance, informed with jouissance, an image of jouissance. A very desiree of a novel. (7)*

Makarand Paranjape (born August 31, 1960), is a poet, critic, novelist, short-story writer, literary columnist, and reviewer with an enquiring mind that has resulted in his publishing seminal articles and books. Currently a Professor of English at Jawaharlal Nehru University's Centre for English at the School of Language, Literature and Culture Studies, New Delhi, India, his creative writing signals a new Indian literature that is polished and thoughtful. He has edited or authored about thirty-five books and published more than 100 academic papers both in India and abroad, in addition to poems, short stories, and more than 250 periodical essays, reviews, and other publications. Paranjape has organized and coordinated several international conferences. He has also been an invited speaker and presented academic papers all over India and in over fifty countries abroad. He has been a Homi Bhabha Fellow for Literature (1991-1993) and held visiting appointments/ fellowships at several institutions including the Indian Institute of Advanced Studies, Carleton University, Iowa University, University of Texas-Austin, Ball State University, University of Sao Paolo, Federal University of Minas Gerias, Murdoch University, Autonomous University of Barcelona, the Oxford Centre of Hindu Studies, and Universitat des Sarlandes.

Makarand Paranjape, one of India's most prolific writers, has to his credit four published collections of poetry—*The Serene Flame* (1991), *Playing the Dark God* (1992), *Used Book* (2001) and *Partial Disclosure* (2004). Apart from this he has written short stories that have been featured in publications ranging from *Femina* to *Debonair.* These stories have been collected in a volume called *This Time I Promise It'll Be Different* (1994). Paranjape even has a novel to his credit, *The Narrator: A Novel* (1995) and at least one of his books of criticism, *Decolonization and Development: Hind Svaraj Revisioned* (1993) is cast in a dramatic mode. So he is a creative artist of many shades, to say the least. However, Makarand Paranjape's debut novel *The Narrator: A Novel* is altogether a different kind of creative endeavour and what follows is an analysis of Paranjape's novel in the light of psychoanalytic criticism, chiefly within the framework of the main ideas of Freud and Lacan and also highlighting the Deleuze and Félix Guattarian model of the schizoanalysis.

The protagonist of Makarand Paranjape's *The Narrator: A Novel* is Rahul Patwardhan, a Lecturer of English at Asafia University, Hyderabad who possesses a complex schizophrenic desire to write a novel but is unable to do so for his belief in literalism and disciplined truth and, in the process has given birth to his libidinal alter ego—the progenitor of all his 'sexploits' and early creativity. It is probably his own uninhibited self—he calls it "Baddy."

> So, as I was growing up, reading voraciously, preparing to be what I always knew I'd turn out—a teacher, a scholar, a boring person—

> a character invented itself, embodying all that I couldn't be. He was called "Baddy." Baddy because he was bad, but also because he was the only real buddy I had. Baddy was also a joke on Freud, whom I had started reading on the sly, with clandestine relish and eager astonishment—Baddy, a sort of variation of Libido. (10)

As the novel begins, we find Rahul undergoing a most curious experience—a horrifying, strange and magical phenomenon: there is a sudden emanation from his mouth, which soon assumes a transparent human shape.

> The emanation finally materialized in the evening. Gradually, it assumed shape and form before my eyes. I was stunned into silence, almost stupefied, an open-mouthed and horrified witness to the strange phenomenon. (1)

The ghostly figure is soon transmogrified into Badri(nath Dhanda), a man with a purpose, a self-made businessman who proposes that Rahul and he should author a film script together to which Rahul with obvious hesitation finally agrees upon. After this, in the course of the narration of a typical Bollywoodian script of *Manpasand*, Rahul and Badri tell their autobiographies—their birth, upbringing, education, profession, libidinal pursuits, most often foregrounding their sexualities. While Badri remains in action, Rahul's other half, Baddy hibernates.

The real-life-narrative is almost parallelled by reel-life narrative where we encounter Tara, a wealthy, beautiful and ambitious young woman, the heroine of the filmy script who haunts for a "suitable boy" with her actress friend, Mohini. We also encounter a host of other characters—Vilas, a private detective and also the hero, Osman a poor photographer, Syd an underworld don, Bhusan, the designing drunkard together with a host of other minor characters that make up the cast of *Manpasand*, "a rip-roaring romantic comedy-cum-gangster film" (Kumar 211). This filmic storyline becomes more fascinating and remarkable with the interpenetration of the "reel" life and "real" life: the creators of the script, both Rahul and Badri make a brief but significant appearance in their own film to set things right in the end: "We are the authors of this story. We are like mythological deities who guard over our favourite characters. This is our cameo appearance" (236). And when Rahul and Badri intrude into their own script of *Manpasand* as the principal protectors, Tara breaks the boundaries of narrative framework of the film *Manpasand* and enters the main narrative of the novel itself. When Tara makes a comment about Badri's sexual behaviour, which is known, only to Rahul and the real readers, Badri asks her, "So you've been reading this book too, have you?" (244) and Tara says: "You wrote the book in which I was a character; can I not at least read the book in which you are a character?" (244). And Makarand Paranjape, in one of his short stories, hints at the possibility of such kind of interchangeability saying, "Sometimes real people walk into stories. But sometimes, stories also walk into the lives of real people" ("Fact or Fiction," 107). Thus, the life of Rahul and Badri, the story of the film *Manpasand*, the doings of the actors and narrators, Rahul, Badri and Tara, the going on of Baddy get mixed up; the thin demarcating line between text and sub-text is fused (Das 70-71). And finally, Rahul's long innings of tensions, trials and tribulations ends with the birth of a little daughter, Amen.

The narrative of *The Narrator: A Novel* is a mishmash of several stories woven together and presented to us from viewpoint of several writer-narrators or character-narrators. In the words of Badri,

> The Indian story is never a straightforward narrative, marching tidily from the very beginning, through the middle, to the end. Rather, it is like a labyrinth or the whorls of a flower. It is multilayered and multilinear. (274)

However, the central concern of the novel is to represent a potential writer's anxiety about the making of a narrative or a novel.

Rahul Patwardhan, the protagonist, embodies the anxiety of arriving as a writer.

> I, Rahul Patwardhan, lecturer in English at Asafia University, Hyderabad, the husband of Neha, the friend of Badrinath Dhanda, and the "other" of Baddy, would like a chance at rewriting my own character. (246-47)

Rahul has a rich fund of creative imagination manifest through his creative self, Baddy but lacks contact with reality or real context. Rahul, therefore, eagerly waits for the arrival of his worldly self—Badri who supplies him with realities of life—the raw material for his imaginative literature. Badri takes Rahul to enter the world of naked, shocking realities of incest, homosexuality, communal violence, prostitution, corruption, inhumane exploitation and hypocrisy rampant in the socio-political environment of India. Badri is Rahul's "other"—the subject's experience of his "I", a component of a "self" that is internally divided. But Badri is also, at the same time, Rahul's the "big Other"—other subjects whom the individual encounters in social life; and for Lacan it also stands for language and the conventions of social life organized under the category of the law. Thus, without Badri, Rahul cannot grow as a human being let alone a writer.

Lacan sees the unconscious as structured by language, but consisting of language only at the level of the signifier, not the signified. In this respect, the unconscious allows for the free play of language as sign before it is trained into specific, fixed meanings or signifieds through conscious processes (Felluga). Related to this is Lacan's model of the construction of the individual subject in childhood which passes through two crucial stages: the "mirror" stage and entry into the "symbolic order." This reinforces the "desire" to adopt a language outside oneself and an image of oneself is conferred by borrowing a language which exists outside oneself; and this "desire" in the Lacanian term is "the desire for the Other" (Webster 92). Thus in Lacan's scheme of things, that which introduces "lack" and "gap" into operations of the subject is the "other"; and in its "otherness," in its exclusion from the imaginary, it is the cause of lack which initiates "desire" for entry into the "symbolic order."

In Paranjape's *The Narrator: A Novel*, the protagonist, goes through the Lacanian psychodrama: Rahul's aspirations to become a writer, to write a novel which "is intelligent in form, self-conscious in technique" (7) are tied up with Lacanian notions about the Real, lack, desire, and movement from the Imaginary to the Symbolic order. Rahul's personality is fragmented, dispersed and decentred. Rahul's disease-creative schizophrenia shatters him into three parts—Rahul: Baddy: Badri—and this tangle is a constant source of tension and suspense in the novel. Rahul's basic problem is that he is enmeshed in divergent pulls of desire and his awareness of various kinds of lack. These go into the making of his otherness and a general unease of otherness always surrounds him. Here is a passage which points to the lack of a neat fit between the signifier and the signified:

> Long ago, when I was about fifteen, I realized that I could never write such a novel. The realization was as sudden as it was devastating. It caused unbearable anguish and forever, so to speak, split my personality. Perhaps, this break with my ego-ideal might have occurred even earlier when, as a child, I would be suddenly afflicted with afflatus. I would rush about confused, driven, restless, trying to create something—anything that could salvage my pride, salve my unspeakable desire. But, in the end, fail—miserably and totally, returning to myself depleted and forlorn and defeated. . . . So at fifteen I came to a conclusion that given who I was, given my mind and its limitations, I could never be the creator of the desired opus. (7)

Rahul seems to suffer from creative schizophrenia but at the same time constantly feels the presence of his creative self—Baddy who inspires him to write poems.

Rahul's vacillation or movement from one signifier to another—Rahul: Baddy: Badri—might be interpreted as a symptom of what Lacan means by desire. The split parts of Rahul's being embody desire as well as a lack which has desire strives continually to fill. Rahul's language works by such lack i.e. the absence of real objects which signs (words) designate (Kumar 218). The first part of the novel is inspired by Baddy who also narrates the story of Rahul's writing self but he vanishes when Badri, Rahul's worldly self arrives.

> Badri was in reality what Baddy was trying to be in imagination. Badri had actually lived a very rich, diverse, and interesting life, full of poetry, sorrow, and adventure, which Baddy was merely trying to conjure up for his unwritten novel. . . . With him [Badri] around, I didn't really need Baddy (93).

So, it is through the character of Badri, the marginalized, the oppressed, the subaltern, that Rahul makes a return to the centre in the society.

Badri takes Rahul by his nose and acquaints him with the sordid realities of life. With Badri, Rahul has the advantage of experiencing life without actually having to live it. Naturally, a character like Badri often uses a native-variety of English and a lot of Hindi idioms in his rather down-to-earth conversations and that too with panache. For instance, when the fellow-waiters at Papaji's Dhaba taunt him: "Sala padne chala hai. Pata nahin apne aap ko kya samajhta hai" (31) or when he says of his mother, "She had been repeatedly, er, molested. . . . Un ki izzat lut gayi thi" (20) or the flood of four-lettered Hindi words while recounting his victimization as a "sex" object by his uncle and his cousin (41). At the same time, it is through the mouth of Badri that we come across (Paranjape's) sophisticated theories of fiction, narratology or characterization. It is astonishing how an uneducated man like Badri could display the finesse exhibited in arguments like the art of story-telling (274-75), or on the deconstruction of Baddy-Badri duo (263) or on sexual politics (253-55). Thus, Badri becomes not only Rahul's (or Paranjape's) alter ego, but it is also through Badri that the society's language is used to give a sense of Rahul's individual identity. Hence, Rahul acquires an identity within the symbolic order; and once the act is complete, Badri disappears from the life of Rahul when half of the script of *Manpasand* is yet to complete and reappears only when his presence is an unavoidable one for the completion of *Manpasand*. "Badri appears from nowhere and disappears into nowhere. He changes the narrator's life, though like a catalyst. Throughout, multiple interpolations are possible. Badri never existed: or both Badri and Baddy exist but cancel each other out" (263).

However, according to Lacan, the Real is the irreducible surplus of the 'outside world' that resists being turned into language as the Symbolic or into spatial representation as the Imaginary. The Real, in Lacanian terms, is by definition inaccessible. Neither the Imaginary nor the Symbolic can fully comprehend the Real, which remains out there somewhere, but beyond reach because beyond the subject and beyond representation (Selden, Widdowson, & Brooker 168).

It is to be contrasted with *reality*, a field heavily structured by Imaginary identifications overlaid by Symbolic signifying chains. Hence, the filmy script, *Manpasand* produced by the protagonist Rahul as also the novel written by his creator Paranjape might be interpreted as the Real, and not a *reality*. *The Narrator: A Novel* is itself a critique on the form and technique of novel and it needs to be further analyzed how far Paranjape has been able to transform his theory into practice. And the writer himself admits, "I had tried to market it abroad, but had failed. . . . In India, my book had a lukewarm reception. There were a dozen or so reviews, but it faded away rather quickly. I was not entirely happy with *The Narrator*, though I believe that it has much more going for it than some of its reviewers have thought. I had attempted it more like an exercise than a real work of art" (Paranjape, 2009, 164).

Makarand Paranjape's *The Narrator: A Novel* can also be analysed from Freudian perspective. Badri himself in the novel does the psychoanalysis of his relationship with Rahul:

> If Rahul is Oedipus, the repressive embodiment of authority, the representative of the enslaving political and economic forces, then I am the Anti-Oedipus, who innocently and brutally ruptures this mechanic suppression of libidinal energy. I provide the interruption to the continuous coding mechanism of society. (279)

Sigmund Freud understood the mind as constantly in conflict with itself, and understood this conflict as the primary cause of human anxiety and unhappiness. Freud's investigations into internal conflicts led him to an eventual division of the mind into three parts, three conflicting internal tendencies, the well known id, ego, and super-ego. The id comprises the unorganized part of the personality structure that contains the basic drives; the id acts according to the "pleasure principle." The ego comprises that organized part of the personality structure that includes defensive, perceptual, intellectual-cognitive, and executive functions; the ego acts according to the "reality principle." The super-ego comprises that organized part of the personality structure, mainly but not entirely unconscious, that includes the individual's ego ideals, spiritual goals, and the psychic agency, commonly called the "conscience" or the "morality principle" that criticizes and prohibits his or her drives, fantasies, feelings, and actions; the super-ego aims for perfection. According to Freud, the creativity wells up from unconscious drives, i.e., the id, which is the repository of repressed sexual and other unwanted libidinal desires. However, the id, as we know, is always in conflict with social standards of morality, i.e., the superego. The ego or the artist has special power to negotiate these insatiable demands of id and censoring dynamics of super-ego. Thus, a work of art, to Freud, is a disguised fulfillment of a suppressed or repressed sexual wish (Sharma 119-80).

Makarand Paranjape's *The Narrator: A Novel* reveals an excess of eroticism or sexual aberrations. There is sex all around, in all its variations of softness and crudity—straight in Badri's desire for Tara, innocent homosexual love involving Rahul and Jerry, hetero in Badri involvement with Firdaus, incest as exposed in Meena's interest in Badri, sodomy as explicit in Badri-uncle relationship, mental adultery in Rahul's explanation of Baddy's birth and his sexploits, extra-marital in Rahul-Jenny affair, child abuse by Badri's maternal uncle, voluptuousness as experienced by Rahul in the brothel and prostitutes like Suzannah, Shanti, and others, and pure love as depicted in the marital relationship between Rahul and Tara. Paranjape makes his point very clear when the readers find Badri proclaiming:

> sex is one area in which the modern man is most confused and complexed. . . . This other side to sex, the selfish, violent, irrational, and painful side, is brought out into the open here. Some people are likely to wonder why not a single sexual encounter here is beautiful, elevating, happy. Well, why should it be that way? The rest of the world is busy glorifying and mystifying sex; why should it bother anybody if the uglier, but perhaps more real, side of sex is also exposed now and then, not in some social welfare report, but in fiction? (254-55)

However, this is not merely an erotic or romantic novel dealing with sex. Paranjape intentionally crafts the narrative to be an erotic as he has a definite purpose in his mind. The novelist is self-conscious of his pornographic project and its consequences. He sees these sexual aberrations very natural but finds them repressed, forbidden and conflicting with the bourgeoisie "censor" that is pushing them back in unconscious as these do not fit in society's standards of morality and propriety. The novel can be seen as a liberator of libidinal fantasies and "vile bodies" (Chaturvedi, para 2). And, of course, its effort to include all variations on the matter of sex has a very serious subtext of sexual/ textual politics.

Nevertheless, Freudian model of id, ego and superego can be handful to analyze the character of the protagonist Rahul. Rahul is an artist who is caught between the incessant sexual drives of Baddy, the storehouse of the libidinal energy (pleasure principle) and the morally constraining, tutored nature of his good self, the Lecturer in English at Asafia University (morality principle).

In case of Rahul Patwardhan, he is a schizophrenic kind of person. He is split between 'Goody' and 'Baddy' Rahul. While talking about his past life, Goody Rahul declares himself as Mr. Clean and blames Baddy Rahul for his amoral and wayward adventures of life. It appears that the narrator who is talking with Badri and who is narrating the script of "Manpasand" is Goody Rahul. But the climax comes when Goody Rahul realizes he has been murdered by Baddy Rahul since Goody can't be a writer. So, Rahul Patwardhan is doubtful about his ability as a narrator. He is trapped in two minds and unable to locate the role of the narrator (Jarandikar, para 5).

The conflict between Baddy (id) and his good-natured self (superego) is so destructive that Rahul has developed schizophrenia. And, here emanates Badri (the ego of the artist) who allows the artist Rahul to overcome the conflict and repressions. Badri, similar to the functioning of ego, manages to mediate the transgressive demands of Baddy and the limits imposed by his good-natured self. The script *Manpasand* he narrates to Rahul which is finished by Rahul, in a way, shows the special ability of the artist to shift the original libidinal drives from their sexual orientations to non-sexual higher goal (a movie script). The result is a 'fantasized wish-fulfillment' for the artist Rahul and a mode that releases the tensions of his schizophrenic self opening the way back to reality, to his wife and the baby.

To conclude, Paranjape seems to prefer Deleuze and Félix Guattarian model of the release of the libidinal energy rather than the Freudian concept where the artist uses the mechanisms of condensation, displacement and symbolism. Paranjape re-eroticizes the latent sexual desires of Rahul when towards the end of the novel, he encounters a British *femme fatale* Jenny and enjoys sex with her though the event is contrived deliberately and self-consciously to parody the East-West cross-cultural encounter which stays as a sine qua non of Indian writing in English (Kumar, 212). Paranjape does not consider sublimation or purging off the bodily desires essential to alleviate schizophrenia of the writer/narrator Rahul.

Contrary to the neuroticising process of psychoanalysis, Paranjape re-eroticises Rahul freeing him for his libidinal pursuits in opposition to the repressive regimes of the conscious which territorialise and control individual sexual desires from being allowed their freedom. Instead, he unchannels and 'deterritorialises' Rahul's desires to produce 'a body without organ' (Chaturvedi, para 4).

Following Deleuze and Félix Guattarian model of the schizoanalysis, Paranjape construes a fragmented, liberated, libidinal body of Rahul—a model for liberation from the restrictive binaries through creatively positive mode of writing. Thus, the "schizophrenia" that Deleuze and Guattari embrace is not "a pathological condition" but "a positive process"—expansion rather than withdrawal (Massumi 1). This opening out or expansion of Rahul into Baddy and Badri facilitates him to express freely, to create. Schizophrenia here becomes a rhetorical trope to write a fiction helping the narrator to become a writer by the end of the narrative. Rahul's aspiration of becoming a writer is fulfilled by the end of the narrative—the manifesto of a writer anxious to arrive as a novelist is satisfied. What Rahul (as well as his creator, Paranjape) achieves ultimately is a novel which is "intelligent in form, self-conscious in technique . . . a novel born of jouissance, informed with jouissance, an image of jouissance. A very desiree of a novel" (7)

Works Cited

Bhatnagar, M.K., ed. *Indian Writings in English.* Vol. II. New Delhi: Atlantic, 1998.

Chaturvedi, R. "Self as Narrative in *The Narrator: A Novel*: A Narratological Perspective." *The Criterion: An International Journal in English* 2 (1), 1-8. http://www.the-criterion.com/V2/n1/ Rahul.pdf, 2011.

Das, B.K. *Postmodern Indian English Literature.* New Delhi: Atlantic, 2003.

Felluga, D.F "Modules on Lacan: On the Structure of the Psyche." *Introductory Guide to Critical Theory.* http://www.purdue.edu/guidetotheory/psychoanalysis/lacanstructure.html, 2011, Jan. 31.

Jarandikar, N. *Search for Narrator in The Narrator: A Novel.* http://www.makarand.com/reviews/ReviewsofTheNarrator.htm, 2006.

Kumar, Sudhir. "Who is afraid of Postmodernism? Reading Makarand Paranjape's *The Narrator: A Novel* in the context of theory and practice of Postmodernist Fiction," *Indian Writings in English,* Vol. 2, ed. M.K. Bhatnagar. New Delhi: UBSPD, 2001.

Massumi, B. *A User's Guide to Capitalism and Schizophrenia.* Cambridge: The MIT Press, 1992.

Paranjape, M. *The Narrator: A Novel.* New Delhi: Rupa, 1995.

______. Welcome to Makarand.com! http://www.makarand.com, 2010.

______. *Another Canon: Indian Texts and Traditions in English.* New Delhi: Anthem Press, 2009.

Selden, R., P. Widdowson, & P. Brooker. *A Reader's Guide to Contemporary Literary Theory.* 5th ed. New Delhi: Pearson, 2005.

Sharma, R.P. *Insights into Literary Theory: Eastern and Western Perspectives.* New Delhi: Gyan, 1996.

Webster, R. *Studying Literary Theory: An Introduction* (Second Edition). London: Arnold, 1996.

Aravind Adiga's *The White Tiger*: A Reading of the Novel in the Light of Hegel and Nietzsche's Concepts of Master-Slave Relationship

ANUP KUMAR DEY

Aravind Adiga's debut novel The White Tiger *presents an unattractive portrayal of India rattled by poverty, underdevelopment and corruption. The novel is also an interesting study of the master-servant relationship which may be analyzed from the context of Hegelian Master-Slave Dialectic as well as Friedrich Nietzsche's concept of Master-slave morality. Hegelian dialectic talks about the encounter between two self-conscious beings in a "struggle to the death" until one enslaves the other only to find that it does not give him his desired result. Again Nietzsche is of the view that there are two fundamental types of morality: 'Master morality' and 'slave morality'. Master morality weighs actions on a scale of good or bad 'consequences' unlike slave morality which weighs actions on a scale of good and evil 'intentions.' In this novel Adiga has portrayed his protagonist Balram Halwai which has the potential of provoking interpretations from the aforesaid two contexts.*

Aravind Adiga's debut novel, *The White Tiger*, was first published in 2008 and won the Man Booker Prize in the same year. The novel presents an unattractive portrayal of India rattled by poverty, underdevelopment and corruption. An epistolary novel developed through a series of letters written over a period of seven nights by its protagonist Balram Halwai explores the realities of two Indias—rural and urban—and depicts a contrast between familial allegiance versus self-determination, individual choice and responsibility, identity determined by caste, class and religion, and the impact of globalization. The protagonist who identifies himself as a white tiger is writing these letters to Chinese premier, Wen Jiabao, during late hours of nights under the scattered lights of chandelier telling the tale of his life and his rise from the son of a rickshaw puller of a dark village to a successful entrepreneur in a modern city. During the course of his journey he has to pass through different stages of his life—a teashop waiter, an apprentice driver and mechanic, a chauffeur as well as a massager in the house of a wealthy man, a murderer as well as a wanted man and finally a manipulative entrepreneur.

The story Balram tells starts with his life in Laxmangarh, the village of darkness in northern India. Being the son of a rickshaw-puller he can not expect his family to support him to finish school. In spite of having the sign of a good student appropriate for a rural Indian school he, instead, is forced to break coals and wipe tables in a teashop and earns money to be sent to his grandmother. He is even deprived by his family of a distinct name as he is simply called by the name "Munna," a very common name of millions of children in India which simply means "boy" in Hindi. It is his schoolteacher Mr. Krishna who at the time of entering his name in the school register names him Balram in reference to the name of the elder brother of Krishna, the most revered god in India. His surname, Halwai, points out his social standing as it refers "sweet-maker" in the caste system (56).

In his letters, while reminiscing his past, Balram calls himself "half-baked" (11) who despite possessing the potential recognized by the school inspector, who praised him as an "intelligent, honest, vivacious fellow," a 'white tiger', "the rarest of animals—the creature that only comes along once in a generation" (35) has to sacrifice the prospect of a scholarship and proper schooling and has to work at a teashop to earn money for marrying off one of the daughters in the family. In rural India, the family elder decides the fate of other members and lays claim to most of their earnings and the case of Balram is not an exception to this. But being a smart guy he anticipates a better future which takes him to Dhanbad where he learns driving. Eventually after marooning for some days in search of a proper employment he skilfully manages to get close to a rich man from his village known as "The Stork" because of his fondness for taking "a cut of every catch of fish caught by every fisherman in the river" (24) who hires him as a chauffeur. This becomes a turning point in his life and he is set to play multiple roles as chauffeur, servant, massager, cook etc.

Balram cunningly becomes the chauffeur of the younger son of the family Mr. Ashok and his wife Pinky madam and comes to live with them in Delhi and the city turns out to be a new revelation for him. As he drives his master and his wife to shopping malls and other parts of the city, Balram gradually becomes aware of immense possibility and opportunity that the city may render him and he becomes increasingly worldly and ambitious and thus one may notice the gradual change of his behaviour and nature from "the Country-Mouse" to a city rat and a kind of subversion of the traditional master-slave relationship.

Master-slave relationship in India is a complex affair where a servant is expected to perform all possible roles demanded by the master—from an orderly to bring whisky from wine shop to a close associate who can be trusted with millions of rupees. He is expected to perform the roles of a gardener, a sweeper, a cook, a massager as well as an expert chauffer who can fill up the empty glasses of his masters sitting on the back seat while driving. It is also expected from a good servant to understand his master's mind as he should arrange things as wished by his master in different situations. The servant also becomes a specimen to display the ignorance of millions of people living in rural India as Mr. Ashok tries to hold a picture of ignorant Indian masses to his wife who returned from America by putting simple questions and in getting wrong replies (sometimes deliberately done by Balram in order to please his master). If circumstances demand he is also expected to take the blame of the master of running over the pedestrian on himself. In that case the traditional master-slave relationship is somewhat altered as he is granted promotion from sitting on floor to a couch and is offered tea and snacks. But if the situation is somehow averted, he has to go back to his earlier standing.

The master-slave relationship in case of Balram and Mr. Ashok is somewhat different from the traditional one as the latter tries to find solace in the company of the former when he is torn between the expectations of his family to take over the household business by staying back in the country and the overimpending pressure from his wife to return to America. Mr. Ashok even alters the norm and goes to the servants' quarter and sits on Balram's bed and talks to him in a friendly voice. Even when he tries to beat Balram after the latter drops his wife to the international airport to leave him forever, he does not seem to be motivated by the traditional practice of ill-treating servants; his action can be analyzed as a momentary reaction against a frustrating situation. But this somewhat different type of master-slave relationship between them also undergoes change when "mongoose," the elder brother of the family comes.

Balram tries to explain the reason of Indian servants being so honest by calling them Rooster Coops (175). In spite of having the maximum opportunity of robbing their masters an Indian servant will not take advantage of the confidence of his master when it really matters; although he may indulge in minor cheating like earning some extra bucks by way of selling fuel, providing inflated service bills or by turning the cars into passenger vehicles unaware of their masters. The novel is an interesting study of the master-servant relationship which may be analyzed from the context of Hegelian Master-Slave Dialectic as well as Friedrich Nietzsche's concept of Master-slave morality.

The Master-Slave dialectic (*Herrschaft und Knechtschaft* in German) is a famous passage of Hegel's *Phenomenology of Spirit* (1977) which is considered a key aspect in Hegel's philosophical doctrine. This dialectic talks about the encounter between two self-conscious beings in a "struggle to the death" until one enslaves the other only to find that it does not give him his desired result. To elucidate how it works, Hegel tells a story about how two people meet. But Hegel's concept of the development of self-consciousness from consciousness, and its sublation into a higher unity in absolute knowledge, is a phenomenological construct. The master-slave dialectic can be interpreted as an internal process occurring in one person or as an external process between two or more people. What occurs in the human mind also occurs outside of it. The objective and subjective, according to Hegel, sublate one another until they are unified and when two contradictory moments result in a higher unity.

According to Hegel, the first encounter of two abstract consciousnesses results in astonishment at the realization of the self as an alien object. Each one of the consciousnesses tries to ignore the other which hinders in the formation of self-consciousness and each considers the other simply as an animated object rather than an equivalent subject. Otherwise, they become enthralled by the mirror-like other and try, as done earlier in controlling their own body, to assert their will. According to Hegel, "On approaching the other it has lost its own self, since it finds itself as another being; secondly, it has thereby sublated that other, for this primitive consciousness does not regard the other as essentially real but sees its own self in the other." (Hegel 111)

The "I" sees another "I" and feels a kind of threat to its own supremacy and command and tries to ignore this other. The only way of re-asserting itself, so as to advance toward self-consciousness, is by entering into a struggle for supremacy and consequently the struggle to the death ensues. However, in case of death of any one between the two, the realization of self-consciousness fails. In Hegelian terminology this failure is "abstract negation" not the negation or sublation required. This death can be avoided either by the agreement, or by subordination, or by communication, to slavery. In the course of this struggle for supremacy, the Master emerges as Master because he is not afraid of death as much as the slave and the slave, out of this fear, consents to the slavery. In later course of the dialectic this experience of fear on the part of the slave is important for his further development as it forms the prerequisite experience. Only in the case of survival of both, recognition of self-conscious is achieved and this recognition of the other gives each of them the objective truth and self-certainty required for self-consciousness. Thus, it helps the two in entering into the relation of master/slave and simultaneously preserves the recognition of each other.

However, full self-consciousness can not be achieved at this state. The master's self-consciousness is dependent on the slave for recognition as he works to shape nature into products for the master. The slave, through his creativity, creates more and more products with greater sophistication and gradually he realizes that the world around him is created by his own hands which ultimately makes him to feel associated with his own labour and thus achieves self-consciousness. But as the master depends wholly on the products created by his slave he is enslaved by the labour of his slave. The realization of this alteration of role makes the slave to struggle against his master once again. It is resolved only when the difference between the slave and the master disappears with the recognition of equality by both master and slave.

The White Tiger is an interesting study in the context of Hegelian Master-Slave dialectic as it operates at different levels. Balram Halwai comes to the house of "the Stork" to take up the job of a chauffeur. Before joining here he has already displayed his skilful nature of manipulation as well as cunningness and it should not be expected that he has come here only for the sake of earning some bucks to support his family in the village. The master-slave encounter begins with the sense of supremacy on the part of the master and a sense of hatred on the part of the slave as he holds an adverse opinion regarding his master since his childhood. So, the process of ignoring the entity of the slave starts with the incident of scolding Balram for overhearing the conversation of his masters and engaging him to do other works not supposedly to be done by him. It also reflects a kind of suppressive mechanism to negate the identity of the slave as a human being against which Mr. Ashok, the younger son of the master who has recently returned from America, raises a docile voice which is squashed by his father and the elder brother. On the other hand Balram also ignores the entity of his master and cherishes a kind of desire to subvert that relationship and his mentioning of his masters as "the stork" and "mongoose" vindicates it.

Balram is well aware of the fact that on the way to his freedom from slavery and reaching to the state of self-consciousness the greatest hurdle is his confinement in the household of his masters. So he grabs the chance of accompanying Mr. Ashok and his wife to Delhi as their driver by skilfully ousting the old driver. He anticipates it well that the new city may bring him new opportunities on the way towards freedom. Again the Hegelian master-slave dialectic is operational in the novel where the master enjoys the supremacy as Balram follows every instruction of his master without putting any question. He is even ready to take the blame of running over a pedestrian on himself in order to save his master. But it does not mean that the master-slave relationship in the novel has avoided the Hegelian "abstract negation" as the penultimate act of killing of his master by Balram and his act of running away with the money frustrates the process of achieving self-consciousness in him.

It is also a fact that the relationship between Mr. Ashok and Balram is somewhat close to the stage of the recognition of the self-consciousness as the former has reduced the gap between them by way of sharing his feelings with him and even by showing unconventional gesture of sitting on his torn bed in the decrepit dark room of the servants' quarter. Being frustrated by the prevailing corruption in Indian politics and business as well as by a not so supportive wife, Ashok finds in Balram a close associate who can be trusted with money as well as in other respects. By now Balram has matured enough to feel that he can stand alone outside the orbit of his master and can create his own space. But the dependency of Ashok on Balram is in a way in conformity with Hegelian master-slave dialectic which is again subverted by the act of Balram's killing of his master.

The White Tiger may also be analyzed from the context of Friedrich Nietzschè's concept of Master-slave morality. Master-slave morality is a central theme of Friedrich Nietzsche's works particularly in the first essay of *On the Genealogy of Morality* (1973). Nietzsche is of the view that there are two fundamental types of morality: 'Master morality' and 'slave morality'. Master morality weighs actions on a scale of good or bad 'consequences' unlike slave morality which weighs actions on a scale of good and evil 'intentions.'

For Nietzsche, master morality is the morality of the strong-willed; while slave morality values things like kindness, humility and sympathy, master morality values pride, strength, and nobility. Unlike master morality which is sentiment, slave morality is literally re-sentiment—revaluing that which the master values. This strays from the valuation of actions based on consequences to the valuation of actions based on "intention". (Nietzsche 63) As master morality originates in the strong and slave morality originates in the weak it is a reaction to oppression and it condemns its oppressors. Slave morality does not try to transcend the masters, but to make them slaves as well. The essence of slave morality is 'utility' (Nietzsche 122): the good is what is most useful for the whole community, not the strong. Nietzsche saw this as a contradiction, "And how could there exist a 'common good'! The expression is a self-contradiction: what can be common has ever been but little value. In the end it must be as it has always been: great things are for the great, abysses for the profound, shudders and delicacies for the refined, and, in sum, all rare things for the rare." (71) As the strong-willed are few in number, the weak acquires power by corrupting the strong-willed into believing that the causes of slavery are 'evil.'

The story of Balram Halwai is actually the study of Nietzsche's concept with a difference. In it the master-slave morality is turned around culminating in the killing of the master by the slave. As Nietzsche points out essential qualities like pride, strength, and nobility in master morality, we find the first two qualities in the two masters, "the stork" and "mongoose," whereas nobility is missing in them. It is vindicated in their various actions in the novel; particularly the lack of nobility in "mongoose" is displayed in his act of shifting the responsibility of running over a pedestrian from his sister-in-law to Balram. On the other hand Mr. Ashok and his wife lack the first two qualities although possessing a considerable amount of the third one. It seems that the strong-willed master morality has been shifted from the master to the slave as Balram displays more of it than his master. Moreover, Nietzsche's view that the slave morality values things like kindness, humility and sympathy are uncharacteristically missing in Balram and some other members of his family. The act of his grandmother in taking him out from the school and pushing the young boy in the unfavourable world to earn for the family is a clear example of lack of these values. Moreover Balram's selfish act of sacrificing his entire family against the wrath of his masters for the sake of money also confirms it. Even at the fag end of the novel, the indication of blackmailing by his nephew for the sake of ice cream (316) points out the clear lack of these so-called values of slave morality. Thus the novel *The White Tiger* has the potential of provoking many other interpretations.

Works Cited

Adiga, Aravind. *The White Tiger*. New Delhi: HarperCollins India, 2008.

Hegel, G.W.F. *Phenomenology of Spirit*, trans. A.V. Miller. Oxford: Clarendon Press, 1977.

Nietzsche, Friedrich. *Beyond Good and Evil*. London: Penguin, 1973.

Ecological Degradation and Identity Crisis of the Minority: A Study of Rohinton Mistry's *A Fine Balance*

DIPANKAR CHAKRABARTI

We have started, newly, to understand the ecological problem and its impact on the human habitation after the Rio though we have, by the time, lectured a little more than our real concern. The attitude of the colonial people regarding the development of minority people more or less remained unchanged even during the postcolonial period. The newly emerged nation-states were engaged in consolidating their domains and steps were taken to assimilate and assert control over 'minorities' and 'tribal groups.' It soon became clear that independence from colonial control did not automatically mean a liberation for the oppressed ethnic groups within the new states.

The basic sense of eco-literacy tells us that the very existence of human race depends mainly on the environment as the race survives as long as earth survives in its present form. Man draws upon components of his natural and societal environment to sustain his various activities which, in turn, have impact or repercussions on the components of his environment. It is the appropriate attitudes, values and life styles which may be the most important determinant in judging the quality of human activity. People can transform and re-evaluate their priorities, and principles, so that the quality of life is enhanced and the environment can be disciplined and well-manned.

The greatest enemy of any ecology is, perhaps, the civilization itself. The whole world today is in the grip of 'development'—the meaning of which or its direction, however, remains obscure. Under the shade of Globalization, extreme consumerism has commodified natural objects. The socio-economic dynamics based on a 'single vision' of the gradual economization and rationalization of the earth renders us susceptible to 'Nature's Revenge'—the convulsions of natural system struggling away from our grasp. The resources of a 'potential eco-system' are seen, so far, as mere a purveyor of a resource capable of being extracted for 'maximum sustainable yield.' The market signals may also, propel decision-makers in the arenas into harvesting the profit from a system that 'on paper' sounds healthy, but in fact on a downward ecological spiral. In lieu of the cauldron of competing 'worlds,' our time is increasingly under the spell of 'one world formulas'—formulas backed up by the hegemonic status of Western societies and world views. The formula converts the planet into a world without alternatives and diversity—and hence without hope or vision. But to the forest-dwellers, in general, land is not a private property but a god given nature's gift—not to be sold or bought. In independent India, the pattern of land use had been so organized as to maximize the revenue it yielded and the commodities it could produce to maximize the economic gain. Countries, as ours, looked upon the indigenous people as 'biotic pressure' and dubbed these ecosystem-people as 'anti-development, retrograde rabble-rousers' and opponents to be destroyed in order to make material advances. But, in fact, it is the commercial demand of the omnivores that stonewalls all attempts at sharing with ecosystem-people because Native ways of perceiving and dealing with life derive from an ecosystemic, anthropocentric perspective on the world. The concentration of capital incentive activities in the countries favouring narrow elite of omnivores at the cost of masses of ecosystem people has created a large number of ecological refugees in countries like India. Like the colonial powers these 'biosphere people' not only enjoy the produce of the entire biosphere but also claim it as their right, in contrast to the ecosystem people who have a very limited resource catchment.

As in Latin America and Africa, strong voices of dissent are raised against the one world formula even in India. The root cause of this dissent is the indiscriminate overexploitation of resources by the developing countries violating the basic principles of environment. Exploitative societies generally violate the basic principles of environment and in these societies, 'development is generally taken to mean the utilization of natural resources mainly to meet the luxury consumption requirements of a relatively small section of population' (Dogra 187). This section has political, economic and muscle power and they use it ruthlessly for accumulation of riches as well as a life of consumerist abundance. In this pursuit they generally show scant respect for any adverse effect likely to be caused to the other people; to the livelihood of the minority people and to the sustainability of their natural environment and the lifestyle they are pursuing. Both the developed and the developing nations follow, more or less, the same development policy which, in turn, displaces the indigenous minorities from their natural habitats. The Cobo Report (1982-83) detailed how the right of the indigenous minority especially tribal peoples throughout the world were being squashed. The report also testified the existence of word-wide persecution, forced resettlement, the denial of legal assistance and land rights and the imposition of culturally destructive and genocidal policies. Now-a-days these indigenous minorities are becoming more and more conscious of their rights and are 'fighting to overcome the shadows that dog their collective existence' (Colchester 32). It is in this context that the problem of environmental degradation of minority population of the word, particularly in India, vis-à-vis development programmes and policies of the respective countries deserve serious attention.

Though the I.L.O's Convention 107 recognizes the rights of indigenous minorities and tribal populations to the individual and communal ownership of their traditional lands, even in India the rights of the estimated 70 million Adivasis to their collective ownership of their land remain largely unrecognized and most of them are subjected to respective forestry laws which place them at the mercy of local forest departments. The fundamental thread of connectedness with the nature and natural of the forest-dwellers is denied. Culturally violated from the others, perhaps, as a result of postcolonial fractures, these indigenous people are more attached to land and forest. Loss of land has deprived them of the main source of livelihood. And as a result the primitive minorities, in this pseudo-civilization, stand as an untold history of a marginalized, dispossessed and besieged culture.

In India, the Adivasis were pushed out of their natural environment mainly because of our adherence to Western notion of development. Among the other factors which resulted in making the indigenous people ecological refugees most important of them is, perhaps, the denial of land ownership and rights. Traditionally the tribal in India had built a culture and societal structure that ensured a happy balance between human and ecological needs. Colonial Policy during the British Raj in India saw to it that both the raw-materials requirements of the colonizing country and the revenue needs of the colony were met exclusively through indigenous resources, initially through land and later through other means. But as the land owning upper class became politically important, land tax could not be raised. The tribals, on the contrary, had no bargaining power whatsoever and posed least threat in terms of reprisals to British rule. Thus their forest system could be attacked with impunity. Revenue from forests could be obtained primarily through the sale of timber. Consequently the revenue orientation of the colonial administration essentially led to deforestation. This trend of using forest as a source of resource continues also after the independence. To this are added the raw material requirements of forest based industries that have come up as a result of planned development.

In comparison to their Western counterparts, the South Asian Canadian writers have treated man-nature relationship in their works from a completely different perspective. Particularly, for these writers coming from a warm country like India, the Nature in the mountainous region is considered to be more human-friendly than in the arid and desert region. As such Eastern attitude towards Nature is based more on caring and sharing. But the influence of the Western culture especially their emphasis on technology and development has become the chief cause for the environmental degradation and ecological crisis in a country like India. Such ecological crisis in the South-Asian countries demands an altogether different approach with a view to deal with the destructive effect of modernization based on consumerism and industrialization and the consequent existential crisis. Among the current brood of South Asian writers in Canada, Rohinton Mistry has dealt elaborately with this aspect of ecological and environmental crisis in his fiction.

In *A Fine Balance*, Mistry has, as is evident, portrayed a few characters' relationship with the Nature around them with utmost sensitivity and depth. Most of these characters belong to his own Parsi Community, which is an ethnic minority in a predominantly Hindu India. Thus the existential crisis, mainly due to the partition and its subsequent after-effect in the form of massive ecological degradation which they confront in their personal, social and national life constitutes the central concern of the novel. The protagonist Farokh Kohlah is a victim of the partition of India in 1947, a ruthless and selfish imposition of British colonizer:

> A foreigner drew a magic line on a map and called it the new border; it became a river of blood upon the earth. And the orchards, fields, factories, businesses, all on the wrong side of that line, vanished with a wave of the pale conjuror's wand. (205)

Though denied of the vast family fortune, Farokh along with his wife Aban and little son Maneck continue to relish life in the foothills meeting their needs from the small left out general store. In addition to this Farokh had been handed over a secret soft drink formula by his father, popular as Kaycey and quite a rage among the small town people. Though his wife's people living in a city by the sea beseeched them periodically to leave the mountain and move over to their place, Farokh and his family continue to live in their ancestral home in the hills praising always, 'The air and water is so pure, the mountains so beautiful' (209). Like his father, son Maneck too loves his home in the mountain to such an extent that his temporary departure for the city for education makes him nostalgic. Even a streaming bowl of water in the bathroom brings to his mind the vision of the dreamy mist that would be hugging the mountains in the morning:

> at this hour it would be swirling fancifully, encircling the snow-covered peaks. Just after dawn was the best time to observe the slow dance, before the sun was strong enough to snatch away the veil. And he would stand at the window, watch the pink and orange of sunrise, imagine the mist tickling the mountain's ear chucking it under the chin or weaving a cap for it. (201)

Though Farokh had lost one of his eyes in an accident while bottling Kohlah's Cola and wore an eye patch on it, on his long evening walks though the hillside forest he would put it in his pocket and admire for the umpteenth time the beauty of the place. His wife Aban too enjoyed the magnificent view of the valley from the back of the general store. Not only for Farokh and his family, but for his friends like Major Grewal and others also the mountain was a part of their life, like a living intimate persona as if they lived together side by side. However their harmonious relationship with the nature was soon disrupted by the government's plan to connect the hill town to the cities. They who never dreamt of leaving the mountain were shocked to find the mountain leaving them. Mistry's subtle and veiled criticism is candid enough to target the self-styled messiahs for the development of the nation: 'These were to be modern roads . . . roads that would hum with the swift passage of modern traffic. Roads wide and heavy duty, to replace the scenic mountain paths too narrow for the broad vision of nation builders and World Bank officials' (215).

Threatened by the forces of modernization and urbanization which would eventually destroy the green mountain and the environment of the hill-town, Farokh and his friend Major Grewal organized a meeting to condemn 'the flawed development policy, the short-sightedness, the greed that was sacrificing the country's natural beauty to the demon of progress' (215). They sign petitions and lodge their protest with the authorities, and wait. To their utter dismay, the authorities, those messengers of development equipped with the western ideas of technology and urbanization turn a deaf ear to their fervent appeal. The road continues to inch upward, swallowing everything on its path. The invasion of technology is presented by Mistry quite evocatively:

> The beautiful hills by its side become gashed and scarred. From high on the slopes, the advancing tracks looked like rivers of muds defying gravity as though nature had gone mad. The distant thunder of blasting and the roar of earth-moving machines floated up early in the morning and the dreaminess of the dawn mist turned to nightmare. (216)

More than anybody else Farokh Kohlah is shocked to the core of his heart. He feels as if he has been displaced from his dear land once again. The devastation of nature around him makes him depressive and terrified. His mental state finds expression in the following lines:

> Mr Kohlah watched helplessly as the asphalting began, changing the brown rivers into black, completing the transmogrification of the beloved birth place where his forefathers had lived as in paradise. He watched powerlessly, while, for the second time, lines on paper ruined the Kohlah family. Only this time it was an indigenous surveyor's cartogram, not a foreigner's imperial map. (216)

Ironically enough, the nation's plan primarily deprives him of his family fortune but holds out the promises of increased business in the second place. But in its promises lurks the venom of modernization which would deprive him of the family's name and his sense of identity. He complains to his wife bitterly that 'the noxious exhaust from the lorries was searing his nostrils and the ugly throbbing of their engines was ripping his eardrums to shreds' (217). Along with the pollution of air and noise, which is primarily one cause of ecological imbalance, the so-called modernization brings in hordes of job-seekers who live in shacks and shanties by the slope of the hill and defile the environment through the defecation and devour the forest for firewood. Farokh is shocked by a permanent stench of human waste that hung in the mountain air and to see 'bold patches upon the body of the hill.' As though, corresponding to the protagonist's feelings of convulsion and anguish, the nature too reacts sharply against the technological invasion unleashed upon it, as Mistry writes:

> Then the seasons revolted. The rain which used to make things grow and ripen descended torrentially on the denuded hills, causing mudslides and avalanches. Snow, which had provided an ample blanket for the hills, turned skimpy. Even at the height of winter the cover was ragged and patchy. (217)

Farokh felt a perverse satisfaction at nature's rebellion. It was a vindication of sorts: he was not alone in being appalled by the hideous rape of the environment. But the seasonal disorder continued year after year only to break him deep down inside. Taking a walk in hills, the long solitary rambles which were the greatest pleasure to invigorate him, now seemed like a death watch. Haunted by the continual loss of the trees and rocks of the dearest mountain where he belonged, Farokh desperately looks for them:

> Coming upon a favourite tree, he would stop under its branches a while before moving on. He would run his hand along the gnarled trunk, happy that an old friend had survived another day. (217-18)

The menace of modernization causes ecological imbalance and consequently, an existential dilemma for Farokh. While the people's comments about the disillusioned protagonist, 'Mr Kohlah's screw is getting a little loose. He speaks to trees and rocks and pats them like they were his dogs' (218) brings out his mental state, it also impresses upon us his desperate search for his old place in the lap of nature. At this juncture Mistry's portrayal of the protagonist is that of a knowledgeable, sensitive and spiritual person based upon idealism and traditionalism, while the generation of people around him stand out in stark contrast as ignorant, insensible and materialists charged with spirit of modernization and change.

Finally, it was a heart-rending vision of the sunset during his walk on the hillside that conveys to Farokh the inevitable message he was so desperately waiting for:

> Suddenly he noticed that dusk had fallen: the sunset was forfeit behind the pall. And the entire scene was so mean and squalid by the twilight, so utterly beyond his ability to accept or comprehend. He felt lost and frightened. Waves of anger, compassion, disgust, sorrow, failure, betrayal, love-surged and crashed, battering and

confusing him. For what? Of Whom? And why was it? If only he could. (218)

Unable to make out the myriads of confusing emotions, Farokh feels a tightness in his chest, then his throat constricts as if he were choking. He weeps helplessly, silently venting his emotions. The meaning that this vision gives him is too new and terrifying for him to explore. There is no place for escape and he realizes that 'his dreams had succumbed, during their collision with the passing years. He had struggled, he had won, he had lost. He would keep on struggling.' (219)

A further bout of displacement catches him unaware, through modern material force of consumerism. Their technique of 'hard-sell' and cut-throat competition targets to overtake the sell of his family soft drink, Kaycey, forcing it to the brink of close-down. Though his son Maneck, being modern generation young man welcomes the idea of changing and improving the general store, Farokh looks for his identity in the restoration of the past. He has an honest and touching reply about the consumerist culture and its garbed language like 'hard-sell': 'What kind of a language is that? Sounds absolutely undignified. Like begging. Those big companies from the city can behave like the barbarians if they want to. Here we are civilized people.' (220)

The modern generation has no place for such traditional and old-fashioned men and no honour for their sentiment. By his resistance to modernization and change, Farokh loses both his son and his own place in the scheme of a transmogrified homeland.

The final wish of Farokh after his death speaks volumes about the intense shock and anguish he had undergone by the invasion of modernization and its accompanying forces like consumerism and technology. Disillusioned by the way his dearest homeland in the hills was devastated and defied, he wished to be cremated and to get his ashes scattered in all the difficult places and terrains of his dear hills. Primarily, his wish for cremation was an outraging one as his religion Zoroastrianism prescribes the disposal of dead body by feeding it to vultures. Anticipating that any left out part of his body might further defile the land, he even dares to violate the sanction of his religion. Furthermore, by the consummation of his final wish with scattering of his ashes over the hills and the valley, Farokh seeks his lost identity through complete assimilation with his dearest trees, rocks and hills.

Man interacts with nature through the medium of culture. It is the culture, which provides the values and knowledge for man-nature interaction. Mistry's message in this regard is quite candid and radical. So long as the cultural values are sensitive to ecology, man's relationship with Nature remains harmonious and cordial. But when we adopt cultural values alien and unsuitable to our environment lured by its superficial and glamorous façade, a vicious circle of destruction and decay is unleashed, whose swift currents wash down the life-sustaining elements of nature. 'Modernization and development through technology and science,' a concept of the western culture is not an unwelcome idea. Rather, Mistry seems to suggest that its mindless execution without proper introspection and planning, would adversely affect Nature, thereby creating ecological and existential crisis. Through his elaborate and sensitive presentation of man-nature relationship. Rohinton Mistry stands out as another spokesperson of Ecological movement.

Like most developing countries, India too, as may be safely assumed, has taken it for granted that industrial growth as the pattern set by the advanced nations of West is the only course open to it. Consequently Indian Development policies geared to 'resource utilization rather than resource conservation' has become the primary concern for the Governments and has led to environmental degradation. Instead of playing the role of 'preserving space for the under privileged 'as well as 'protecting people and cultures from globalizing trends,' and striving to reduce poverty and the promotion of equality what is happening around us is the Indian state apparatus' itself becoming an instrument of oppression by being captive to the privileged elites and thus becoming an accomplice in marginalizing the minorities. The Indian middle class is progressively adapting itself to the global bourgeois in the process of abandoning social conscience in favour of borrowed notion of development, vulgar commercialism and relentless pursuit of private health and pleasure. Together with the commercialization of the forest which has led to its destruction, external values have entered in the minority society. Constructive dependence of the minorities is thus gradually replaced by destructive dependence. Ours is the time of re-evaluation of the values of the individualism inherited from the previous centuries and European Enlightenment tradition. There is a new viewing of the earth in terms of *human community* where environmental sensitivity and working together are clearly seen as pathways and answer for current global and ecological problems. Cardinal draws us into this debate in his style of working and philosophy of architecture. He argues that aboriginal culture works in contrast to the materialism and acquisitiveness of modern industrial society. He, rather, supports the idea that we should uphold a system that emphasizes life-style, ethical and new moral values whereby the human being is re-integrated into the fabric of community and towards environmental sensitivity. He points to native and tribal values of *community* which are being re-emphasized by native people. In this re-evaluation, there is a *wholism* that is indigenous to the ancient way of conceiving the connection of humankind with nature. This sense of the communal feeling is deeply associated with sensitivity of human individual needs. Identity of the aboriginal minorities is never threatened. To ensure a green civilization he prefers to generate a tie with landscape, ecology and minority feeling.

NOTES

1. The term 'minority' is used as a broad spectrum with an apolitical meaning, simply to mean the representation of their human resource to an existing population-density irrespective of geographical / global barrier. Naturally all ethnic/non-ethnic groups comprising both tribal/non-tribal and indigenous/ non-indigenous groups are assimilated in the term. As most of the forest dwellers are indigenous communities their matters are specially stressed in the study.
2. Ecosystem people: The (aboriginal) group of people who by their way of living profitably participate in a potential ecosystem.
3. Biosphere people: The parasitic bourgeoisie community fed on the by-products of a potential ecosystem

Works Cited

Cardinal, Douglas. 'Structural Geometry,' *Canadian Architect*, Vol. 29, No. 10, Oct.1984: 30-33.

Dogra, Bharat, ed. *Encyclopaedia of Development, Environment and Welfare*. New Delhi: Bharat Dogra, 1995.

Marcus, Colchester. 'A Native Renaissance,' *Down to Earth* (June 15) 1996, 32-37.

Mistry, Rohinton. *A Fine Balance*. London: Faber and Faber, 1996.

Indian Novel in English: An Epoch Making Genre: Agent for Socio-Psycho-National Reforms

ADWITIYA GOPE

Throughout its long history, the genre, novel has evolved by way of stylistic and formal innovation, taking advantage of the genre's elasticity to try new approaches and new techniques. Nevertheless Indian English novel writers, down the ages, made use of this genre to their own ends. Novel form became machinery for Indian writers in English to address multifarious issues related to nationalism. The argument of the paper is that the Indian novel writers of English write back in this genre to uphold the intense issues related to nationalism.

The novel started flourishing in the eighteenth century England with Daniel Defoe's *Robinson Crusoe* and Jonathan Swift's *Gulliver's Travels*; and with Jane Austen became the preferred entertainment of the middle class. The form of this genre got little out of hand during the 1920s and 1930s with Joyce's *Ulysses*, Faulkner's *Sound and Fury*, Woolf's *Jacob's Room* but soon it settled back. And today our best novelists follow in this great tradition: that is realistic narratives driven by a strong plot and peopled by well-rounded characters struggling with serious ethical issues, conveyed in language anybody can understand. Throughout its long history, the novel has evolved by way of stylistic and formal innovation, taking advantage of the genre's elasticity to try new approaches and new techniques. Nevertheless Indian English novel writers, down the ages, made use of this genre to their own ends.

Q.D. Leavis in her classic *Fiction and Reading Public* (1932)documents British reader's immense affection for the genre. She reports that novels comprised one-third of the total holdings in British public libraries in the late nineteenth and early twentieth centuries, they were requested over four times more often than works of non-fiction. From this, Leavis remarks: "Considering that the II percent minority which takes advantage of its right to borrow books from the public libraries is probably the more enterprising section of the poorer reading public, (this) shows convincingly enough the supremacy of fiction and the neglect of serious reading which characterize the age." (4)

It is considerably the 'supremacy' of fiction in mid-to-late-19th century Britain that bred the neglect of 'serious' reading in the twentieth century. It is precisely so that the novel evolved in the East much as it did in the West and pretty much along the same timeline. The objective of this paper is to study that the emergence of the novel in India in English from its introduction under the aegis of 19th century British colonial policies through the 1980s, worked as agency for socio-psycho-national reforms. And for that matter this paper would have explorative study of Krupabai Satthianadhan's *Saguna*, Khushwant Singh's *Train to Pakistan*, Salman Rushdie's *Midnight's Children* with occasional references to some other Indian novels.

Although according to imperial zealots such as Thomas Babington Macaulay, the colonizers issued directives and the native, it has been assumed, more or less complied with. Though the English novel in its proper form was introduced in India through colonial agencies, my argument is that Indian novel could manage to rise to a level from where it could seek greater equality with the existing form of the genre in the Britain, thereby manipulating the genre to become a tool to raise mass awareness among its native readers to go for socio-psycho-national reforms and therefore despite this apparent neglect of serious reading as spoken by Q.D. Leavis, Indian novel in English ascended to serious standards.

Despite its colonial legacy, when the Indian novel emerged, it successfully subverted earlier colonial policies and radically reversed the priorities of Englishness and the empire. Gauri Viswanathan in her "Masks of Conquest" (1989) and Ashis Nandy in his *The Intimate Enemy* (1983) do conform to this fact. Ashis Nandy opines that colonized Indians soon create an "alternate language of discourse" to British colonialism which he identifies as "their anti-colonialism" (xvii). And this fervour of anti-colonialism which in turn responds to nationalism gets reflected in the works of Indian novel writers down the ages.

As nineteenth century India remained increasingly under the British influence and dominance, the colonial hegemony in India came into being first through a group of London merchants who came to India with an exclusive trading purpose in the early part of the century, then taking the possession of the country to be ruled by the crown and the parliament of England by the end of the century. So, British indulgence in India moved through trade to taxation, education to administration and from occupation to the ultimate target of ruling the country. As in this period, English language and English ways prevailed in India, many Indians did not regard the English influence as altogether a bad influence nor did they abjure it. My paper would argue that in this realm of mixed reactions, some Indian novelists well conversed in English, showed their skill in using English language, "alternate language of discourse," as spoken of by Ashis Nandy, to address the very issues of socio-psycho-national reforms.

Nationalism in Novel of Colonized/Pre-Independence India

Krupabai Satthianadhan (1862-1894) is regarded as the first English woman novelist in India. Though the first Indian novels began appearing in regional languages in the late 1850s and

1860s, Satthianadan's English novels *Kamala* and *Saguna* (1895) turned out to be an epoch-making genre that could address some of the most intense issues surrounding narratives of nation, empire, tradition, gender and, above all, the emergence of English novel in India.

Being a converted Christian Indian woman, Satthianadhan portrayed the crisis created in the-then Indian lives. Satthianadhan's two novels, numerous short stories, and prose sketches appeared in India in the 1880s and 1890s, an extraordinary period as far as Indo-British colonial relations are concerned. Her writings especially Saguna, is punctuated by calls for reform on a number of social and political issues and marked above all in colonial India by multilevel representational crisis:

Crisis created by Christianity
Crisis created by Modernity
Crisis created by Tradition
Crisis punctuated by Nationalism

The strongest force in Satthianadhan's life is Christianity. Every experience in *Saguna* is generally steeped in Christianity. Every crisis is again resolved by it.

In the very first paragraph she talks about the influence of Christianity, which is the theme of the novel:

> In the following pages, I shall in my own way try to present a faithful picture of the experiences and thoughts of a simple Indian girl, whose life has been highly influenced by a new order of things—an order of things which at the present time is spreading its influence to a greater or lesser extent over the whole of her native land." (Satthianadhan 19)

The purpose of her writing is to propagate the "new order." Now the question comes why her father supports Christianity and converts into Christianity, a religion in which Saguna finds solace throughout her life. Saguna's father Harichandra decides to convert because this religion helps to liberate him from orthodox Hindu familial ideologies:

> Some of those with whom he argued could not but acknowledge that Christianity had in it, in a more highly developed form, truths which were only dimly outlined in the Hindu shastras. (55)

Christianity works in their lives as an emancipatory medium. Christianity liberates Radha from the repressions into which Hindu (Brahmin) religious and cultural ideologies as institutionalized in her time have forced her. Once converted, she and her husband build a home in which the new order is the guiding light and driving force. Christianity permits equity in the marital relationship with its profession of the equality of all souls before God: "There was now no feeling of constraints between Haricbandra and Radha." (62)

Satthianadhan's narration of Radha's story with much emphasis on the superiority of Christianity is presented in a mode of religious propaganda and seems to follow the pattern of British missionary women novelists in the 19th century India. Her alignment with colonial machinery is also evident from her description of the landscape of the Deccan:

> We ascended a little rocky eminence, and were looking at the wonders round us, the mists and the shadows, and the play of the light overall, when suddenly the scene changed, and the sun emerged from behind a huge rock. In a moment the whole place was bathed with light. . . . My brother in his usual earnest way remarked that it is just like this, shadowy, dark, mystic, weird, with superstition and bigotry lurking in every corner, before the light of Christianity comes into a land. When the sun rises, he said, all the glory of the trees and the rocks comes into view; each thing assumes its proper proportions and is drawn out in greater beauty and perfection. So it is when the sunbeams of Christianity dispel the darkness of superstition in a land. (22-23)

Thus, Christianity which comes in India with the Colonial masters helps a section of people to emancipate from orthodox superstitious Hindu custom.

The dawn of modernity was guaranteed with the advent of colonial machinery in India. During the late 19th century, with the advent of modernity, the woman-question takes a new turn. Now a woman who aspires to be "New Woman" wants to be educated, seeks equality between men and women, and wants to create a new identity for herself. To get all these, the first and foremost pre-requisite is education. We find Saguna trying her every bit to get herself educated. Early in her life, Krupabai's elder brother Bhaskar began to "direct her thoughts to learning, showed her what books to read, infused new ideas into her and told her much about great men, heroes, patriots, philosophers and about Greece & Rome" (20)During that period, education was something restricted for women. So, she faces opposition:

> My mother, good in her own way, thought that I would be terribly spoiled by having such freedom and learning things that were of no use to a girl. She used to call me to help her with the cooking, which I did not at all like, and would say: 'what a girl you are to go and trouble your head with books! What is the use of learning for a girl? A girl's training school is near the chool (the fire over which everything is cooked), and however learned a girl may be she must come to the chool. (20-21)

But then Krupabai rebels like an Indian Simon de Beauvoir with true feminist resentment against such traditional disparities made between men and women. She says:

> And am I not as good as a boy? I can do as many sums as they . . . and I can read and write too. . . . I only wanted to learn with them, and now they are going to have a teacher. Must I not go and learn too? (76)

Saguna really reaches out to get her identity as a 'new woman' who believes in her own self and tries to be independent:

> I would now throw aside the fetters that bound me and be independent. I had chafed under the restraints and the ties which formed the common lot of women, and I longed for an opportunity to show that a woman is in no way inferior to a man. How hard it seemed to my mind that marriage should be the goal of woman's ambition, and that she should spend her days in the light trifles of a home life, live to dress, to look pretty, and never know the joy of independent and intellectual work! The thought had been galling. It made me avoid men, and I felt more than once that I could not look into their face unless I was able to hold my own with them. (131)

About marriage, she declares: "I don't want to get married. . . . Marriage is not the goal of every girl's ambition." (149) Nevertheless Saguna is aware of the social norms and finally conforms to the set-norms deciding to marry the person her sister and brother-in-law have chosen for her.

The women's questions, in turn, intersect with commentaries on nationalist discourse. Although inspired by Victorianism, Satthianadhan was directly engaged with Indian nationalist discourse of the later 19th century which emphasized the retention of the 'distinctive spiritual essence of the national culture,' as spoken of by Partha Chatterjee in his essay "The Nationalist Resolution of the Women's Question" (Sangari 238). Satthianadhan acknowledges her debt to the west for inspiring the Indian New Woman, but insists that she emulates the 'Aryan' woman traditionally celebrated not only for her self-reliance, but also for her 'shakti' (her spiritual strength) and for her feminine roles within the home unaffected by the profane activities of the materialistic (western) world. Thus she withdraws into Indian history for a suitable feminist mould consistent with her New Woman. By doing so, she attempts to carry on India's own stream of feminism that had been submerged by interactions with other cultures and the gradual degeneration of Hinduism, rather than aping recently introduced western concepts.

Through *Saguna*, Satthianadhan wanted to visualize what India truly was in the contemporary Indian society. *Saguna* being the first Indian English novel by any Indian woman, represents multifarious crisis created in the Indian lives. But deep down the surface level Satthianadhan makes interesting use of the genre (which she has adopted from British people only to use it for her own end) to show her dissent against all colonial machineries thereby raising the intense issues related to nationalism at its heights.

Nationalism in the novel of Partitioned India

Undivided India, which freed itself from colonial yoke and the subsequent partition of the subcontinent are inextricably bound together. Hence postcolonial Indian life could not ignore the pervasive influence and impact of the partition on contemporary life. Novelists of the time could not help themselves but inevitably used novel to express their angst on partition. Khushwant Singh's *Train to Pakistan* (1956) is worth mentioning here to be read as a challenge to any notion of a homogenized post-independence Indian nation. The study of *Train to Pakistan* will re-examine that definition of Indian nationalism is not homogeneous in nature but for obvious reasons it is heterogeneous.

Being the first partition novel to be published in English in 1956, it has undergone vigorous dissections by scholarly critics down the five decades. Though Khushwant Singh in his *Train to Pakistan* depicts the carnage in the Punjab in 1947 with ruthless realism, he is not completely taken up with just the violence for he also redeems a sense of faith in essential humanity at the end of the novel through the figure of Jugga. Nevertheless, the scholarly faculty of the writer is mention worthy as he could exploit the genre to depict realistically the aftermath of partitioned India as it must have been very difficult to take such a stance at a time when the novel was written.

Beyond the level of realism, the novel also functions on an entirely symbolic level. Khushwant Singh uses symbolism to locate three Indian communities in the novel. Symbolism in this novel is extraordinarily important, particularly if the novel is read as Sikh-centred narrative. In this novel, Singh places the Muslims in a position below that of the Sikhs but above that of the Hindus. The effect of this can be read as promoting Sikh hegemony. By emasculating the Hindus in this novel, Singh contests their right, both as individuals and as a religious or cultural group, to inherit the nation India, and in doing so challenges the notion of an exclusively Hindu India. Although Hindus are the majority community in India, their role in this novel is made to be a peripheral one. From the beginning of the novel, Singh sets out to marginalize all Hindu characters that appear in the novel.

In what is almost the opening scene of the novel, the Hindu moneylender, Lala Ram Lal, is seen attempting to hide behind the two women in his house when Malli and his gang of dacoits come to rob him:

> "Open you son of fornication, or we will kill the lot of you," he shouted.
>
> A woman's voice answered. "Who is it who calls at this hour? Lalaji has gone to the city."
>
> "Open the door and we will tell you who we are or we will smash the door," the leader said.
>
> "I tell you Lalaji is not in. He has taken the keys with him. We have nothing in the house."

The men put their shoulders to the door, pressed, pulled back and butted into it like battering rams. The wooden bolt on the other side cracked and the doors flew open. One of the men with a gun waited at the door, the other four went in. In one corner of the room two women sat crouching." (Singh 16-17)

And although after he is found hiding under a charpoy in a room upstairs, he dies without handing over the keys to his safe. The impression the novel creates in the minds of its readers is of a man who hides behind a sari, and who is unable to protect himself or the women in his house. Lala Ram Lal's refusal to hand over the keys appears to be motivated by greed rather than bravery or even a desire to protect his family.

The magistrate and deputy commissioner of the district, Hukum Chand also conforms to this negative stereotype of the Hindu. He too is presented as impotent in the face of violence. He is shown as unable to do anything to stop the train carrying Mano Majra Muslims to Pakistan from being attacked. Instead of taking decisive steps, he is shown to evade his responsibility only by releasing Juggut Singh (a Sikh) and Iqbal (probably a Sikh) from prison in the hope that one of them will be able to prevent the impending massacre; he is powerless to prevent himself. Though the liberated Juggut Singh is shown to have saved the passengers on the train, Hukum Chand's indecision emphasizes the point that, like Lala Ram Lal, he hides behind others.

The only other Hindu male of any consequence in the novel is Mansa Ram, the husband of Sundari, the daughter of Hukum Chand's orderly. The nature of his death is recalled by Hukum Chand towards the end of the novel:

> (Sundari) stopped by day dreaming as the bus pulled up. There were large stones on the road. Then hundreds of people surrounded them. Everyone was ordered off the bus. Sikhs were just hacked to death. The clean-shaven were stripped. Those that were circumcised were forgiven. Those that were not, were circumcised. Not just the foreskin: the whole thing was cut off. She who had not really had a good look at Mansa Ram was shown her husband completely naked. They held him by the arms and legs and man cut off his penis and gave it to her. (203)

Leaving aside the ironic euphemism of the final sentence, it is clear that this passage is designed to show the inhumanity of the mob violence. But significantly it also shows that the Sikhs are allowed to die like martyrs, as Khalsas, with their masculinity intact, while the Hindus are once again emasculated.

Therefore in Khushwant Singh's *Train to Pakistan*, we find desperate negative stereotypical of Hindu community through the characters of Lala Ram Lal, Hukum Chand, and Mansa Ram—may be only to symbolize that post-independence India is not meant for only one particular cultural or religion group (the concept of Hindu India) but the nationalist fervour of the country embraces and provides equal right and space to all its cultural identities thereby shaping only one geographical, cultural, and sociological Nation India.

Nationalism in Novel of Postmodern India

Another novel that examines the concept of nationalism furthermore is Salman Rushdie's *Midnight's Children* (1981). In 1993 Salman Rushdie's *Midnight's Children* was judged the best novel among all the winners of the prestigious Booker Prize in the twenty five years of the prize's history. *Midnight's Children* is considered as the best novel published in the English speaking world outside the U.S. in the last quarter of the twentieth century.

As much analysis and subsequent studies have already been done on *Midnight's Children*, this paper attempts to go for an analysis of the text only to the extent to show that this text exploits the genre 'novel' to raise the issues related to nationalism to a pedestal.

Certainly the story of Saleem Sinai, born at midnight, August 15, 1947, the precise moment at which India received its independence from Britain, has become the central text of Indian literature written in English. Anita Desai recalls hearing the then unknown Rushdie reading from *Midnight's Children* with " a voice that everyone present recognized instantly as being the voice of a new age, strong, original and demanding of attention" (vii). The novel has had an inescapable influence on the succeeding literary generation; and it also occupies a key place in the burgeoning academic field of postcolonial studies.

It is very interesting to note that Rushdie, being an immigrant in the metropole, addressed the issues of how to imagine the nation-state and its history in a world of transnational migration and markets; how to locate oneself in a world of intersecting languages and cultures; how to be postmodern and write from the periphery; and how to make the English language express the needs of Indians. These themes Rushdie first addressed in his own *Midnight's Children.* Saleem Sinai's life is a fictional reworking of Rushdie's own experience as a child in Bombay, living in a house called Windsor Villa, located off Warden Road and overlooking Breach Candy Swimming Pool, with the significant difference that Saleem never leaves the subcontinent and eventually returns to the place where he was born. After adventures that carry him thousands of kilometres from the city of his birth, to Pakistan, Bangladesh, and Delhi, Saleem unlike his creator, retires to Bombay, where a taste of the green chutney that his ayah used to make, has restored the past to him. Saleem does not just remember the childhood self that he had thought long destroyed; he recovers that lost self and is able to do what is denied to most children: return to the care of his ayah. The pickle factory his former ayah now owns provides him with all that he needs in order to pickle his memories and write his memoirs: a room of his own, free time, and an audience on whom to test his writing.

Saleem is a bilingual Indian addressing cosmopolitan readers. His English-language audience is aware of and interested in cultural difference, and willing to be educated about India. They are familiar with the names Nehru and Gandhi, Ganesh and the Quran, but must have Hindi or Urdu translated for them. For their benefit, he is careful to explain that a swastika is "not the Nazi swastika which was the wrong way round, but the ancient Hindu symbol of power" (75), "four annas" make a "chavanni" (134), and Ramzan is "the month of fasting" (178). When Saleem makes allusion to things that are not Indian, for instance, to Karl Marx, Hollywood films, the *Arabian Nights*, or the Bible, he can do so because all these may be found within India. Rushdie invites his readers to see around Saleem. Saleem, the memoirist, is also an allegorical figure for national history. The allegory presumes that the nation can be identified with its political history and that history can be seen as a whole. This perspective is that of the non-resident Indian, who faces most acutely the question of what it means to be Indian and who must look to the map and to national history for an answer. This outside perspective on the state is something new, even in Indian literature written in English, which, before Rushdie, concentrated on the local and the domestic. Explicitly political novels, like *Kanthapura* by Raja Rao (1963) or *Waiting for the Mahatma* by R.K. Narayan (1981), focus on the village or the town rather than on the nation. However in *Midnight's Children* the nation-state is always meant to function on a double perspective, at once a projection of the self on the scale of the world and a means of locating the self within the world.

Conclusion

Jawaharlal Nehru in his magisterial *The Discovery of India*, describes Hindu nationalism as an undeniable but redundant part of the nation's ideological maturing. It was, he stated, "a natural growth the soil of India, but inevitably it comes in the way of the larger nationalism which rises above differences of religion or creed" (240). As nationalism remained 'an undeniable but redundant part of the nation's ideological maturing' (to take Nehru's Concept of nationalism), Indian novel writers of English down the ages have exploited literary genre 'novel' to address issues relating to nationalism. Partha Chatterjee in his book Nationalist thought and the colonial world (1986) defines nationalism as primarily a cultural phenomenon and adds as far as eastern nationalism is concerned, it has drawn its essence from alien cultures in order to become 'civilized.' My argument is that in the process of being civilized, there is risk of losing the nation's own identity. Hence the need for searching a new essence of nationalism prevailed which would regenerate national culture, adapted to the requirements of progress, but retaining at the same time its distinctive essence. These conflicts are addressed by *Saguna*; elaborated by *Train to Pakistan* and resolved by *Midnight's Children.*

Works Cited

Chatterjee, Partha. *Nationalist Thought and the Colonial World* Delhi: Oxford University Press, 1986.

Joshi, Priya. *In Another Country: Colonialism, Culture and the English Novel in India.* New York: Columbia University Press, 2002.

Morey, Peter and Alex Tickell ed. *Alternative Indias: Writing, Nation and Communalism*, Volume 82 of *Cross / Cultures: Readings in Postcolonial Literatures in English.* New York: Rodopi, 2005.

Patel, M.F. *Recent Explorations in Indian English Writings.* Jaipur: Sunrise, 2009.

Roy, Rituparna. *South Asian Partition Fiction in English: From Khushwant Singh to Amitav Ghosh.* Amsterdam: Amsterdam University Press, 2010.

Rushdie, Salman. *Midnight's Children*, New York: Knopf, 1981.

Sangari, Kumkum & Sudesh Vaid, ed. *Recasting Women: Essays in Indian Colonial History.* New Brunswick: Rutgers University Press, 1990.

Sarkar, Sumit. "The Women's Question in Nineteenth Century Bengal." *Women and Culture.* Kumkum Sangari and Sudesh Vaid, ed. Bombay: SNDT Women's University, 1985.

Satthianadhan, Krupabai, *Saguna: The First Autobiographical Novel in English by an Indian Woman*, Delhi: Oxford University Press, 1998.

Singh, Khushwant, *Train to Pakistan.* New Delhi: Penguin India, 2009.

Ten Kortenaar, Neil. *Self, Nation, Text in Salman Rushdie's Midnight's Children.* Montreal: McGill-Queen's University Press, 2004.

Exploring Image-Text Relations in a Post-Independence Indian English Graphic Novel *The Barn Owl's Wondrous Capers*

ARCHITA GUPTA

In the course of this paper, attempt has been made to explore Sarnath Banerjee's The Barn Owl's Wondrous Capers'*s mode of storytelling through image-text combine, and analyse how it tends to write an alternative and non-conventional history of Calcutta with an unfailing sensibility that is Indian. In fact, Sarnath Banerjee has written that his interest in graphic novel genre evolved from a need to redefine and find 'other/ alternative' forms of expression.*

The importance of the Graphic novel genre in Indian context lies in the fact that it depicts 'Indianness' (the axiomatic essence of Indian English literature as a whole) through both text and image (relay and anchorage function as specified by Roland Barthes), since an image can explore the larger realities of life more conveniently. Graphic novel enables contextualization of 'local' space (as against the 'global' and 'national') as is evident in *The Barn Owl's Wondrous Capers* that gives a concrete picture of colonial Calcutta through illustrations. The title is the English translation of Kaliprasanna Singha's 19th century work *Hutom Penchar Nyaksha. The Barn Owl's Wondrous Capers* is simultaneously a postmodern dig at conventional historiography and this paper tends to explore the nuances of this text at multiple levels.

Graphic novel is a recent genre in Indian English fiction. It tells stories with a difference, using sequential art. *Kari* by Amruta Patil, *Kashmeer Pending* by Naseer Ahmed, *Corridor*

(2001) and *The Barn Owl's Wondrous Capers* (2007) by Sarnath Banerjee, *The Hotel at the End of the World* by Parismita Singh have projected the genre of graphic novel to the forefront of post-independence Indian English fiction. The paper attempts to explore Sarnath Banerjee's *The Barn Owl's Wondrous Capers*'s mode of storytelling through the combination of image-text and analyse how it tends to write an alternative and non-conventional / non-canonical history of Calcutta with an unfailing sensibility that is essentially Indian. It gives fictional credibility to certain historical facts in a different way. This paper attempts to explore the text-image relation in the novel at two levels: The level of the 'text'/ textual structure and the level of the theme/ thematic structure

The Barn Owl's Wondrous Capers is essentially a postmodern text conforming to one of postmodernism's chief characteristics that is looking at the past from an ironical perspective, and in the process subscribing to an alternate /subversive genre. The image-text combination of the text is the linguistic/verbal and pictorial encoding that explores the basic theme. The 'text 'itself is complex and generates connotations at multiple levels. Aiming at a more richly layered, dense narrative than *Corridor,* the author succeeds at one of his stated aims, which is to get us to sniff closely at "the dark armpits of history" (1). This being the stated topic, what emerges is an appropriately intriguing material drawn from the old scandals of Warren Hastings' time, the half-explained riddles of the life of Calcutta's founder, Job Charnock. At the textual level, *The Barn Owl's Wondrous Capers* is written in the style of palimpsest where another text effaces the contents of the original text rendering both the text and the narrator a problematic identity. The nature of palimpsest is two-fold; it preserves the distinctness of individual texts, while exposing the contamination of one by the other. Therefore, even though the process of layering which creates a palimpsest was born out of a need to erase and destroy previous texts, the re-emergence of those destroyed texts renders a structure that privileges heterogeneity and diversity and also allows the discerning reader to look into the underlying politics of ecriture and authorly authority at play.

The physical/ original text is interrupted by the pages of the text that the narrator was looking for, thus rendering the concept of 'history' itself problematic. The real text 'The Barn Owl's Wondrous Capers' appears in the end of the novel when the Jew is shown to be reading it (234). It was subtitled 'the dark armpits of history' in the original/ physical text. These two texts intersect at this juncture exposing the authorly authority at play. The palimpsestic nature of *The Barn Owl's Wondrous Capers* reinforces the satiric intent. The subtext is satiric and communicates itself through both the texts—the text of the past and the text of the present. There is a recurrence of a popular history motif—the scandals of society. The authorial intention to bring out the whims, fancies, gossip-mongering, and promiscuity of both the past and present timeframes is explored through the palimpsest mould of the text.

In fact, to understand culture, documented historical fact is not enough, it has to rely on alternate expression such as fiction, visual art, pictures, etc. and the novel does justice to the epigraph that says, "The book is inspired by history but not limited by it" (IV). The very notions of rumour, scandal, popular belief structures, gossip, amorous intrigues and stories of sexual promiscuity that populate popular imagination in any age tend to provide alternative modes of history writing that subvert the grand canonical notion of conventional history. In fact there is a binary/duality embedded in the novel's thematic structure; that of archaeology and history. The quest for the lost book and the act/process of locating it is the archaeological process, whereas the decoding of the ecriture and hence reconstructing the past through the process of reading is the historical process.

The narrator of the second text is the wandering Jew from the past, who makes his presence frequently felt in the novel. The text itself is a dynamic entity travelling in space and time and the novel's thematic structure and the textual structure complement each other.

The basic theme of the novel—the interconnectivity of past, present and future—is facilitated through the graphic novel format that engages the sequence of panels temporally, according to the flow of time. Digital Dutta, the reincarnation of the Jew acts as the link between past and present. The library he owns is a symbol of antiquity. In *The Barn Owl's Wondrous Capers*, time ceases to exist as a static and fixed entity. The present is the shadow of the past. The agency of the spirits and ghosts acts as alternative modes of history reconstructing the untold tales that exist beyond documented history. The presence of spirits or ghosts gives a sense of a real story; re-enacted and dramatized. The choice of this genre is therefore most appropriate.

Theoretically speaking, in film, television, and photography, only one frame is available at a time for the viewer's perception. In sequential art, McCloud writes: "the past is more than just memories for the audience and the future is more than just possibilities! Both past and future are real and visible all around us! Wherever your eyes are focused, that's now. But at the same time your eyes take in the surrounding landscape of past and future!" (104)

In *Time and Space through Sequential Art*, Paul Ricoeur writes: "two kinds of time are found in every story told: on the one hand, a discrete, open, and theoretically undefined succession of incidents (one can always ask: and then? and then?); on the other hand, the story told presents another temporal aspect characterized by the integration, the culmination and the ending in virtue of which a story gains an outline." (427)

Graphic novels convey both the linear and narrative formations of time through the 'sequential art' that is unique to the comic book format. Graphic novels combine text and pictures equally in order to convey a narrative. Both words and images are essential to the graphic novel, thus creating the desire for compatible relationships between visual representation, through skilful art and design, and dialogue or descriptive writing. W.J.T. Mitchell writes extensively on the associations and connections between words and images, "the domains of word and image are like two countries that speak different languages but that have a long history of mutual migration, cultural exchange and other forms of intercourse." (49)

In the successful graphic novel, words and images should be on equal planes, one should not be privileged over the other. One cannot ask of a graphic novel as to which is more important, the words or pictures, as both the domains combine to form an inseparable text. Sarnath Banerjee's graphic novel does the same thing. The satiric depiction of the scandalous history of 19th century Calcutta through his images/illustration and language makes a coherent whole. Graphic narratives are 'performative' in contrast to the typographical text. The text with combination of linguistic/verbal and visual encoding performs for the readers in quite a dramatic mould. *The Barn Owl's Wondrous Capers* performs itself in the living ambience of urban life, false vanities of "the rich colonized and their decadent colonizers" (228). The writer of the book, the Wandering Jew came "here to sell items of whimsy; novelty objects that feed the idle minds of the rich and fuel their active imagination" (229). The pretension of learning and reading was important for keeping one's prestige in the 'elite' society. The humorous and satirical depiction of Joy Mitra's pretended act (pretended as he was illiterate) of reading newspaper in his newly acquired open-top faeton is an apt example of how graphic narrative performs the contents of the text..

The Barn Owl's Wondrous Capers initiates the readers into the days of Babu-culture in British Calcutta. A subversive undercurrent is provided by Babu-Calcutta fringe characters like Gopal Urey and Roopchand Pokkhhi—a device somewhat reminiscent of Nabarun Bhattacharya's *Phyataru*[1] novels in Bengali. The illustrations/images also communicate the varied nuances of characterization. The chapter entitled 'Baghbazaar Bird Club' is full of such illustrative sketches. The Baghbazaar Bird Club whose floors and walls were made of cannabis leaves was famous for the 'smoking ritual.' A panel in this chapter is unique in its presentation of both culture specificity and the satire. The *Khemta*[2] tradition of the then Bengal was performative in its presentation of the scandals through dancing and singing as was the 'Jeleparar shong' (analogous to the 'Skimity Ride' in *The Mayor of Casterbridge* by Thomas Hardy). The panel illustrates the singing tradition, and at the same time describes in a satiric manner the obsession for opium in Bengali Society of 19th century.

Jan Baetens writes that words and pictures are two types of language: verbal and visual. Pictures organized within comic book panels must be perceived as a whole text if a story is to be conveyed to the reader. Through a model of what Baetens calls "relatedness," the panels of a graphic novel are related to one another so as to form "a unified whole." (Saraceni 167).

In graphic novels, the 'text' is formed by the sequence of panels; panels are identical to the sequence of sentences in a text of words, "sentences and panels represent the most identifiable units into which language-based texts and comics are respectively arranged." (Saraceni 169).

Ricoeur explains the process of reading as a process of transfiguration which takes place between the text and the consumer. In Ricoeur's words, "the meaning or the significance of a story wells up from the intersection of the world of text and the world of the reader." (430).

Through reading, the graphic novel consumer is able to access the "fictitious universe of the work" and "reading," which becomes synonymous with "living" in the imaginary mode of existence (432). The advantage of graphic novel as a narrative act lies in the fact that it brings out the cultural specificity of the text through the anchorage[3] text (using Barthes' analogy). The depiction of the Nimtala Cremation Ground and the act of skull cracking in *The Barn Owl's Wondrous Capers*, retain the local culture and specific nuances through the juxtaposition of both, the real photographic image and illustration, so that the act of reading becomes identifying, recognizing and living the moment. Another instance of the intersection of the world of the text and the world of the reader is the anchorage and relay text combination conveying the gastronomy of Hilsa Fish and the familiar scene of the fish market alive in its squalor and mire. Here the image and the text complement each other, both emphasizing /facilitating the narrative intention77.

The axiomatic point of Indian English literature is to construct an Indian space in terms of sensibility, ethos, culture specific stances and geographical/physical delineation. This finds remarkable expression in *The Barn Owl's Wondrous Capers*. Adopting the English translation of Kaliprasanna Singha's *Hutom Penchar Naksha*, Sarnath sketches the eccentricities of 19th century Babu Kolkata. The book *The Barn Owl's Wondrous Capers* that the narrator was searching for is written by the Jew, who supplied what-not to satisfy the whims and fancies of both the British and Bengali elites. The present-day Kolkata is depicted in illustrations as the narrator wanders through the city for the book that is his grandfather's legacy. The uniqueness of Sarnath's illustration is the fusion of real life photographic image and sketches in the same frame thereby blurring the concept of fact and fiction, reality and illusion, conventional history and personal, imaginative history. This could also be read as an attempt to create a sense of the hyper-real—a condition in which the distinction between the real and the imaginary implodes. The photographic image of the Writers Building "the belly button of West Bengal Bureaucracy," "one of the last hubs of authentic babus," "the lasting present from British colonizers" (186) is an example of conventional documented history both in image and text. But the illustration of a babu sitting and delivering the peculiar verbal discourse of babus is an attempt to register personal imaginative history thus creating a blending of fact and fiction. The concept most fundamental to hyper-reality is simulation and the simulacrum. The simulation is characterized by a blending of reality and representation, wherein there is no clear indication of where the former stops and the latter begins. The simulacrum is often defined as a copy with no original, or as Gilles Deleuze describes it, the simulacrum is an image without resemblance. (257).

Essentially, certain historical contingencies allow for wide scale reproduction of simulacra so that the simulations of reality replace the real, producing a giant simulacrum completely disconnected from an earlier reality; this simulacrum is hyperreality (Oberly 4). The creation of the text is one such simulacrum distanced from the original. *The Barn Owl's Wondrous Capers* depicts only one side of a civilization. It is a simulated reality that depicts only the whims and fancies of 19th century Kolkata, the negative devoid of any comments on creativity or freedom struggle in Bengal with the emergence of nationalism. It is also an attempt at the construction of alternate non-canonical history through popular cultural traces.

NOTES

1. A satirical series of fiction by Nabarun Bhattacharjee written in Bengali, acidic in its subversion of modern Kolkata and its culture.
2. A tradition of light song and dance often bordering on the erotic with popular scandals, gossips and rumours as content, performed by nautch girls living on the fringes of society.
3. Anchorage text is meant to "direct the reader through the signified of the image causing him to avoid some and receive others, by means of an often subtle dispatching, it remote controls him towards a meaning chosen in advance" (See Barthes "Rhetoric of Image" 1993). Interrogating the very notion of the anchorage text according to Barthes this paper proposes that in order to ground the semiotic coding/decoding process of the novelist and the readers as well as to communicate intended culture specific stances through graphic storytelling Barthes' definition can be broadened, enlarged and modified to include the graphic /image of graphic novel genre within the category of the anchorage text. This is substantiated by the fact that the graphic narrative performs the same function of 'anchoring' i.e. directing the reader towards a meaning chosen in advance as does the caption in the photograph anchors the meaning of the image, reinforcing the addresser's intended meaning.

Works Cited

Banerjee, Sarnath. *The Barn Owl's Wondrous Capers*. Bombay: Penguin India, 2007.

Deleuze, Guilles. *The Logic of Sense*. New York: Columbia University Press, 1990. 253-65.

McCloud, Scott. *Understanding Comics: the Invisible Art.* New York: Harper Perennial, 1993.

Mitchell. W.J.T. "Word and Image" *Critical Terms for Art History*, ed. Robert S. Nelson and Richard Shiff. Chicago: The University of Chicago Press, 2003.

Oberly, Nicholas. "Reality/Hyperreality 1" *The Chicago School of Media Theory*. <http://lucian-uchicago.edu/blogs/mediatheory/ keywords/realityhyperreality-1/>

Ricoeur, Paul. "Life: A Story in Search of a Narrator" *A Ricoeur Reader: Reflection and Imagination*, ed. Mario J. Valdes. New York: Harvester Wheatsheaf, 1991.

Saraceni, Mario. "Relatedness: Aspects of Textual Connectivity in Comics" *The Graphic Novel*, ed. Jan Baetens. Lovain, Belgium: Leuven University Press, 2001.

Contributors

Professor Somdatta Mandal is Head, Department of English, Visva-Bharati University, Santiniketan.

Sri Partha Sarathi Gupta is Assistant Professor, Department of English, Tripura University, Agartala.

Dr. Somdev Banik is Assistant Professor, Department of English, Tripura University, Agartala.

Sri Bidhan Chandra Pal is Associate Professor, Women's College, Agartala, Tripura.

Dr. Dipankar Chakraborty is Assistant Professor (Senior Scale), Department of English, Govt. Degree College, Khumulwng, West Tripura.

Sri Anup Kumar Dey is Assistant Professor, Department of English, Assam University (Diphu Campus), Karbi Anglong, Assam.

Sri Tomojoy Brahma is Assistant Professor, Department of English, Michael Madhusudan Dutta College, Sabrum, South Tripura.

Ms. Rama Chowdhury is Assistant Professor, Department of English, Bir Bikram Memorial College, Agartala, Tripura.

Dr. Archita Gupta is an assistant teacher working in Maharanipur Higher Secondary school, Teliamura under Govt. of Tripura, West Tripura.

Ms. Banani Chakraborty is a guest lecturer in Ramthakur College, Agartala, Tripura.

Mr. Pratap Deb is a guest lecturer in Ramthakur College, Agartala, Tripura.

Dr. C.L. Khatri is Professor, Department of English, TPS College, Patna.

Mr. Nirmalya Bhattacharyya is a faculty member in ICFAI University, Kamalghat, West Tripura.

Ms. Adwitiya Gope is Assistant Professor, Department of English, Tripura Institute of Technology, Agartala.

Ms. Olivia Sarkar is a ministerial staff in an office under Govt. of Tripura.